MEASURING ACADEMIC LIBRARY PERFORMANCE

A Practical Approach

Prepared for the Association of College and Research Libraries
Ad Hoc Committee on Performance Measures

Nancy A. Van House
Beth T. Weil
Charles R. McClure

AMERICAN LIBRARY ASSOCIATION

Chicago and London 1990

by Stephanie Toral

Text designed by Charles Bozett

Composed by Ampersand Publisher Services, Inc.
  in Goudy Old Style and Helvetica on an Itek
  IGX 7000 Imagesetter

Printed on 50-pound Lynx Opaque, a pH-neutral
  stock, and bound in 10-point Carolina cover
  stock by Imperial Printing Company

The paper used in this publication meets the minimum requirements of American National
Standard for Information Sciences—Permanence of Paper for Printed Library Materials,
ANSI Z39.48-1984. ∞

Library of Congress Cataloging-in-Publication Data

Van House, Nancy A.
    Measuring academic library performance : a practical approach / by Nancy A. Van House,
Beth T. Weil, Charles R. McClure.
        p. cm.
    Includes bibliographical references.
    ISBN 0-8389-0529-3
    1. Libraries, University and college—Evaluation—Statistical methods. 2. Research li-
braries—Evaluation— Statistical methods. 3. Library statistics. I. Weil, Beth T. II. McClure,
Charles R. III. Title.
Z675.U5V35 1990
027.7—dc20
                                                                        89-77253
                                                                        CIP

Printed in the United States of America.

94 93 92 91   5 4 3

CONTENTS

TABLE, FIGURES, AND FORMS

FOREWORD

Accountability has been one of our society's major concerns in the 1980s, with higher education—and, within higher education, academic libraries—scrutinized as perhaps never before. Demands for library accountability come from college and university administrators as well as from legislators and governmental agencies. At the same time, academic librarians are increasingly interested in knowing how well their libraries satisfy users and in gathering data they can use in planning, internal decision-making, and communicating with institutional administrators.

Recognizing that a need exists for analytical tools with which academic librarians can describe their activities quantitatively, the Association of College and Research Libraries Board of Directors created the Ad Hoc Committee on Performance Measures in December 1984, based on the recommendation of the ACRL Task Force on Performance Measures. Two important goals which ACRL wanted to accomplish were to stimulate librarians' interest in performance measures and to provide practical assistance so that librarians could conduct meaningful measurements of effectiveness with minimum expense and difficulty.

Although there is a sizable literature on performance measures, the task force and the committee recognized the need for a practical manual of measures specific to academic libraries. To that end, the committee developed specifications and sought an author for such a manual. Professor Nancy Van House was selected. Along with Beth Weil and Charles McClure, she worked with the committee throughout the preparation and testing of the manual. The measures realize the several goals of the committee—to present instruments or measures which could (1) measure the impact, efficiency, and effectiveness of library activities; (2) quantify or explain library output in meaningful ways to university administrators; (3) be used by heads of units to demonstrate performance levels and resource needs to library administrators; and (4) provide data useful for library planning. The measures are also intended to be replicable in all types of academic and research libraries, to be decision-related, to be easy and inexpensive to apply and use, to be user-oriented, and to be linked to library goals and objectives. The committee and Van House agreed there should be two tests for the manual: first, of the proposed measures themselves in selected academic libraries, and then, when the measures were made final, of the manual itself to determine whether it conveyed what was intended.

Special thanks are due JoAn Segal, then Executive Director of ACRL, and Mary Ellen Davis, Program Officer, for their very valuable contribution and the members of the ACRL Board of Directors for their interest and support. The opportunity to work with a scholar-writer of the caliber of Nancy

Van House—who truly captured the thinking of the committee—was professionally rewarding for all of the committee members.

Ad Hoc Committee
on Performance Measures

Committee members:

Mignon Strickland Adams, Philadelphia College of Pharmacy and Science

Beverlee A. French, University of California, Davis

David Kaser, Indiana University School of Library and Information Science

Patricia M. Kelley, George Washington University

Lynn F. Marko, University of Michigan

Jacqueline M. Morris, Occidental College

Jerome Yavarkovsky, New York State Library

Virginia Tiefel, Chair, Ohio State University

PREFACE

The purpose of this manual is to present a set of practical output measures for academic and research libraries. This manual therefore presents measures that:

- Evaluate the effectiveness of library activity
- Are useful for and replicable in all types and sizes of academic libraries
- Support decision-making
- Are easy to apply and use and inexpensive to administer
- Are user-oriented
- Reflect common library goals and objectives.

An additional goal is to promote the use of measurement for management decision-making in academic and research libraries.

These measures are designed primarily for internal library decision-making, performance assessment, and resource allocation. A secondary purpose is to demonstrate library performance in a meaningful way to university and other parent organization administrators.

The measures are service-oriented. They do not cover the library's internal operations, such as technical services. Instead, they address the quantity and quality of services delivered to users. Technical services provide necessary support to public services; but the measures in this manual are concerned with the service as delivered to the user, not with the many intermediate processes within the library required to deliver those services.

An important service provided by many libraries but not included in this manual is classroom bibliographic instruction. Evaluating instruction requires the measurement of changes in individual skills and knowledge, a different process from that measured by the kinds of measures in this volume. Readers interested in evaluation of bibliographic instruction are referred to the literature that addresses this service, including Knapp (1966), Frost (1978), and especially Bibliographic Instruction Section (1983), which is an introduction to bibliographic instruction evaluation. Chapter 6, "Significant Works," by Richard Werking, summarizes some important studies.

A library should choose from this manual the measures most appropriate to its needs, and not necessarily all of them. The basic questions to ask in choosing measures are:

- What difference will it make for us to have this information?
- Which data will be most useful for the decisions that face us?

Some libraries will want to go into greater depth in specific areas; for these, each measure is followed by "Further Suggestions." References are also made to other literature, as appropriate.

Most libraries will find these measures most useful when replicated periodically, generally every year or two, to track changes. One-time-only data collection will provide useful information about the library's current performance, but this often raises questions about whether service is improving or declining, or the effect of specific library activities, which are best answered with repeated data collection.

The primary audience for this manual is academic and research libraries of all sizes. Very small libraries may lack the resources for the more labor-intensive measures. Larger libraries may have the in-house expertise for more complex measurement. However, larger libraries are often made up of units and branches that, for the purpose of measurement, are much like small and medium-size libraries.

These measures are designed to be used at the service-unit level. A service unit may be a single-outlet library, a branch library, or a service department. For example, in an academic library with a multi-department main library and branches around the campus, data may be collected and analyzed for each branch and for each service department in the main library (e.g., the circulation department, the reference department, the government documents department, etc.).

This manual does not require any knowledge of statistics and requires only very basic math. The methods are explained simply and clearly for librarians whose last math class was many years ago.

This book is in two parts. The first part is about measurement in general. The first chapter introduces measurement in general, and output measures in particular, and their use for evaluation. The second chapter describes basic measurement principles and methods, and the use of measurement in libraries. The third chapter is about user surveys, since several of the measures (but certainly not all of them) require surveys. The second part of the book is a step-by-step guide to each measure, including its definition, the methods for collecting and analyzing data, and a discussion of what each measure means and how it might be used.

This manual was developed by the authors in close consultation with ACRL's Ad Hoc Committee on Performance Measures, which provided the authors with valuable guidance throughout the project. The measures and methods were tested, refined, and retested in a number of academic libraries that generously agreed to serve as test sites, among them, at the University of California, Berkeley:

- BioSciences Library; Beth Weil, Librarian
- Business/Social Sciences Library; Milt Ternberg, Librarian
- Education/Psychology Library; Barbara Kornstein, Librarian
- Environmental Design Library; Elizabeth Byrne, Librarian
- Engineering Library; Camille Wanat, Librarian
- The Library; especially Rita Kane, Associate University Librarian
- Moffitt Undergraduate Library; especially Ellen Meltzer, Librarian
- Public Health Library; especially Tom Alexander, Librarian

Also:

- The University of California, San Diego, Library; especially Ginny Steel
- Shields Library, University of California, Davis; especially Beverlee French

- John F. Kennedy University (Orinda, Calif.) Library; Ann Patterson

The manual was also benefited by our discussions with, and a close reading by, people who took to heart our request that they be ruthless in their criticisms, including:

- Carol Anderson, SUNY Albany
- Loretta Caren, Syracuse University
- Anne Crocker and her colleagues at the Law Library, University of New Brunswick
- Mary Ellen Davis, ACRL
- Henry Lowood, Physics Library, Stanford University
- George McGregor, Cetus Corporation
- Phyllis Mirsky, University of California, San Diego
- Tom Moritz, J. W. Maillard Jr. Library, California Academy of Sciences
- Carol Parke, Syracuse University Library
- JoAn Segal, ACRL
- Jo Bell Whitlatch, San Jose State University

This book has also benefited from the authors' continuing discussions with people who have an abiding interest in library measurement and in bridging the gap between researchers and managers, including:

- Thomas Childers, Drexel University
- George D'Elia, University of Minnesota
- Mary Jo Lynch, American Library Association
- Joey Rodger, Public Library Association
- Douglas Zweizig, University of Wisconsin–Madison

The Council on Library Resources supported data collection for a related project from which this manual benefited.

Edith Balbach created many of the forms in Part 2, patiently enduring endless revisions, earthquakes notwithstanding. She and Stephanie Changaris tested virtually every measure, including the distribution of endless user surveys. Susan Goldstein was very helpful in some of the early stages of the design of the data collection and the forms.

The students in the quantitative research methods class of the UC Berkeley School of Library and Information Studies (Fall, 1989) helped with the collection and analysis of data for the final testing of several measures.

The photographs were provided by Sannita Sutton, J. W. England Library, Philadelphia College of Pharmacy and Science.

The authors are grateful to all of these individuals and groups for their invaluable assistance. Ultimately, of course, the contents are the responsibility of the authors.

## PART I

MEASUREMENT

## Chapter 1

OUTPUT MEASURES IN ACADEMIC AND RESEARCH LIBRARIES

Quality of services is an ongoing concern for academic and research libraries. Indeed, "the single most important challenge facing the academic library manager is securing constructive change and improvement in library performance" (Webster, 1977, p. 83). Improving performance requires information about how good performance is currently, plus feedback on the success of efforts to improve.

Output measures provide objective data on the extensiveness and effectiveness of library services. They quantify library performance in terms of goals achieved and services delivered. These data give staff and management feedback on library performance. They can be used to evaluate the library's services, to demonstrate the library's value, and to guide resource allocation.

The impetus for output measures comes from both within and outside the library. Within the library, the growing use of technology, increasing costs of materials, and the labor-intensive nature of library services all conspire to increase library costs. At the same time, the explosion in the amount of information published and in online access to it increases the demands for services. And as libraries become larger and more complex, management needs objective, standardized data on which to base decisions. Output measures can be used to describe current performance and identify areas where improvement is needed. They can help libraries to allocate resources and plan operations and services. And they can help libraries to assess the success of innovations.

Outside the library, the managers of libraries' parent organizations are increasingly concerned about the rising costs of libraries and other "overhead" services. Funding agencies seek evidence of the library's value and of its cost-effective management. Output measures provide objective data on library performance. And the use of output measures to monitor performance demonstrates the library's concern for efficiency and effectiveness.

This manual is designed to help academic and research librarians to quantify services. This first chapter provides a context for the use of output measures to assess academic and research library performance. It describes a conceptual basis for the development and use of output measures, and discusses the management uses of output measures data. The balance of the manual is devoted to the description and implementation of the measures.

Measurement and Evaluation

Measurement is a tool in the evaluation process. Evaluation consists of comparing "what is" with "what ought to be." Ultimately, evaluation is an exercise of judgment.

Measurement is the collection and analysis of objective data describing library performance on which evaluation judgments can be based. Measurement results are not in themselves "good" or "bad"; they simply describe what is. What these data mean depends on "what ought to be," the expectations or goals that the evaluator holds for the library being evaluated.

Figure 1-1 describes evaluation as a cyclical, goal-based process.

- The first step is the *definition of effectiveness*, the identification of the overall basis for evaluation.
- Then *goals* are established for this particular organization. These goals define what "should be," the standards against which performance is to be judged.
- Based on the definition of effectiveness and goals, *criteria* are developed, which are broad indicators of effectiveness; these criteria are made concrete in *measures*. For example, one criterion of effectiveness may be materials use. This is made concrete in the measures such as Circulation, In-Library Materials Use, and Total Materials Use.
- Ideally, at this point *operations and services* are designed to meet the library's goals.
- *Data* on library performance *are collected* for each measure.
- The data are compared to the goals to *assess library performance*. This is the point at which "what is" meets "what should be."
- Finally, the process cycles back and the evaluators *reconsider* the appropriateness of their definition of effectiveness, criteria, and measures, and their choices of operations and services.

A key point is that the measurement results are compared to the library's goals in reaching evaluation judgments. This manual presents a set of output measures, described in Figure 1-2, to be used to measure academic and research library performance on a set of common criteria, plus instructions for data collection. However, the use of these measures to evaluate library performance, requires that they be considered in the context of each library's goals and circumstances.

Figure 1-1
The Evaluation Process

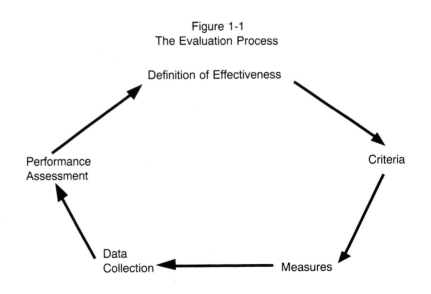

Source: Adapted from Suchman, 1967.

Figure 1-2
The Measures

General User Satisfaction
1. General Satisfaction
   Users' self-reports of success during this library visit on each of several library activities, ease of use of the library, overall satisfaction with today's library visit

Materials Availability and Use
2. Circulation
   Number of items charged out for use, usually (though not always) outside the library. Includes initial charges and renewals, general collection, and reserves.

3. In-library Materials Use
   Number of items used in the library but not charged out

4. Total Materials Use
   Total number of uses of library materials; the sum of circulation and in-library materials use.

5. Materials Availability
   Proportion of user searches for library materials that are successful at the time of user's visit

6. Requested Materials Delay
   Time users must wait for requested material. This may be computed as the proportion of materials requested that are available within x number of days, or as median number of days required to receive requested materials.

Facilities and Library Use
7. Attendance
   Number of user visits to library

8. Remote Uses
   Number of library uses for which user does not come to the library, such as use of document delivery services, access to library catalogs or other online databases maintained by the library from terminals outside the library, or telephone, e-mail, or fax requests for materials or services

9. Total Uses
   Total uses of library, in-person and remote; sum of attendance and remote uses

10. Facilities Use Rate
    Proportion of time, on average, that a facility is busy. Facilities include user seating and workstations and user equipment such as photocopy machines

11. Service Point Use
    Average number of users at a service point. Service points are staffed public service sites: for example, circulation, reference, and information desks.

12. Building Use
    Average number of people in library at any one time.

Information Services
13. Reference Transactions
    Number of reference transactions. A reference transaction is an information contact that involves the knowledge, use, recommendations, interpretation, or instruction of one or more information sources by a member of the library staff.

14. Reference Satisfaction
    Users' evaluation of the outcome of reference transactions, the service experience, and overall satisfaction with the reference service.

15. Online Search Evaluation
    Users' reports of satisfaction with performance of the search intermediary and the search product, and overall satisfaction with the online search.

The Library as a System

Figure 1-3 presents a general systems model of organizations. Its key elements, as they apply to the library, are:

- Inputs: the resources imported from the larger environment (e.g., staff, equipment, and materials)
- Processes: activities that transform resources into a product (e.g., acquisitions, cataloging, reference)
- Outputs: the products and services created by the library (e.g., access to materials, online catalogs, answers to reference questions)
- Outcomes: the effect of library outputs on the larger environment (e.g., the degree to which library use affects students' learning)
- Environment: the larger context which provides inputs, consumes outputs, and affects decision-making in the system. This includes, but is not limited to, the library's parent organization
- Feedback: information from both the system and the larger environment that helps the library improve its processes and outputs and obtain resources.

Inputs are commonly and easily measured, as are many internal processes. Outcomes are the most difficult—perhaps impossible—to measure. The focus of this manual is on the measurement of outputs. Output measures are concerned with the results achieved, not the effort or processes that go into producing them, nor their effect on the environment.

Much library measurement has focused on inputs and processes, on the assumption that more of these will result in more and/or better outputs. This is not necessarily the case, however. Direct measurement of the extensiveness and effectiveness of outputs, when possible, is preferred.

Figure 1-3
General Systems Model

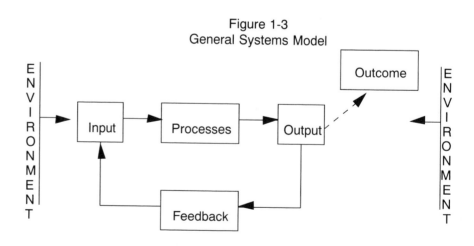

Using Output Measures

Collecting output measure data is only one step in the evaluation process outlined in Figure 1-1. Interpreting and using output measures, like other measurement data, requires a full understanding of the data's meaning and limitations. The discussion accompanying each measure in Part 2 contains information crucial to using the results for decision-making.

Library management and staff must consider these data in the context of the library's resources, clientele, mission, and goals. For example, a large library with a comprehensive collection may aim for a high Materials Availability Rate. Items borrowed from other libraries may be rare and hard to find, so the library may be unconcerned if its Requested Materials Delay shows users waiting a long time. A smaller library, relying heavily on interlibrary loan to supplement its limited collection, may not expect a high Materials Availability Rate but may aim for a short Requested Materials Delay.

Some factors that should be kept in mind when using output measures (McClure, 1986; Van House, 1986; Van House and others, 1987) are:

- A single output measure stresses only one facet of library activity; several measures provide a more complete picture of library services than any one alone.
- Output measures reflect services delivered—uses made of the library. The archival function of the library's collection is not fully reflected. In some libraries, this is a major consideration.
- Conditions can be manipulated to improve the performance on a particular measure without always improving the quality of the service or operation (e.g., one can increase the number of reference transactions per staff member but decrease the accuracy of the answers).
- Measurement results are affected by a number of library and environmental factors. The measures are best used with other information about the library.
- There are no "right" or " wrong" scores on an output measure; "high" and "low" values are relative. The scores must be interpreted in terms of library goals, scores on other measures, and a broad range of other factors.
- Output measures do not in themselves diagnose the causes of inadequate performance. Output measures reflect the extensiveness and quality of service outputs without going into the details of how those outputs were produced. Rather, unacceptable output measures results indicate areas where further investigation or experimentation is needed.
- Much library use is self-service. And when users ask for assistance, they must communicate their needs to the staff and assess the relevance of the information or materials presented by the staff. Output measures reflect user success in the library (D'Elia, 1988G), not simply library performance. The outcome is a function of the library, the user, and the library's success in anticipating the user's needs and assisting in the user's search.
- Output measures results reflect the interaction of users and library resources, constrained by the environment in which they operate. The meaning of a specific score on any measure depends on a broad range of factors, including the library's goals, the current circumstances of the library and its environment, the users, the manner in which the measure was constructed, and how the data were collected.
- At this point, little is known about the factors that affect output measures results. Although we can speculate as to how a library can increase or decrease its scores on particular measures, additional research is needed.

Output Measures, Standards, and Accreditation

The trend in academic library standards is toward a self-evaluation that compares library performance to library and university goals (Lynch, 1986; ACRL Standards for College Libraries, 1986; ACRL Standards for University Libraries, 1989):

> Basic to this document [ACRL Standards for University Libraries] is the proposition that each university library system is unique and therefore should determine its own criteria for performance and evaluation.…[These standards] are not a series of expectations or prescriptive sets of figures. They set forth the process by which expectations may be established, and enumerate the topics that should be addressed (ACRL Standards for University Libraries, 1989, p. 680).

The measures in this manual can be used in developing library objectives and measuring achievement: "This [evaluation] mechanism should establish identifiable outcomes, both qualitative and quantitative, using agreed-upon criteria, and providing appropriate feedback" (ACRL Standards for University Libraries, 1989, p. 685). Those responsible for evaluation should examine the measures in this manual and select those that best reflect the outcomes of interest.

Similarly, the measures in this manual may be used in the self-study process for college and university accreditation to demonstrate the extent and effectiveness of the library's services. Specific measures can be used to demonstrate the adequacy of the library's collection (e.g., Total Materials Use, Materials Availability), information services (Reference Transactions, Reference Satisfaction), and facilities (Facilities Use Rate).

These measures are not suggested as a basis for direct comparisons among academic and research libraries. Such comparisons are not likely to be valid unless the libraries have similar missions and objectives, governance structures, and political settings, and collect and analyze the data in the same manner. As explained in Chapter 2, inevitable local differences in data collection will result in differences in measurement results that do not necessarily reflect differences in library performance.

Previous Approaches

Since the 1960s, as Buckland has noted, "there has been no lack of measures of performance proposed, nor of people proposing them" (Buckland, 1988, p. 241). What has been lacking, however, is tested output measures described with easy-to-use, standardized methods.

A number of writers have made significant contributions to our understanding of the concept of library effectiveness (Orr, 1973; Du Mont and Du Mont, 1979; Du Mont and Du Mont, 1981; Childers and Van House, 1989/90). Some have categorized the range of library services to be evaluated (Orr, Pings, Pizer, and Olson, 1968; Bommer and Chorba, 1982; Cronin, 1985). Others have listed the criteria for good measures (Evans, Borko, and Ferguson, 1972) and reviewed measures that have been used (Lancaster, 1977; Bommer and

Chorba, 1982; Cronin, 1985; and Lancaster, 1988). Two useful international reviews are Goodall (1988), which covers British as well as American literature, and Ralli (1987), which presents an Australian point of view.

An early effort by De Prospo and others (1973) set in place a general framework and practical approach for measuring several aspects of library performance from the viewpoint of the library user. Although specific to public libraries, it was a landmark effort in measurement for all types of libraries in demonstrating that

- library services (outputs) could be measured in a practical manner
- a primary criterion of library performance was the success of users in transactions with various library services
- the quality of services could be measured for a range of libraries that then could compare their performance to similar libraries.

Another notable early attempt was that by Hamburg and others (1974). They extensively reviewed possible approaches to assessing library performance and concluded that the best performance measure for all types of libraries was exposure of individuals to documents of recorded human experience. They translated this to number of uses and time spent with library materials. Many disagreed with this emphasis on document exposure, and the measurement process did not lend itself to easy implementation, but Hamburg's emphasis on the user rather than library resources was influential.

The Public Library Association sponsored the development of a practical manual of public library output measures that built upon the work of De Prospo and colleagues and culminated in *Output Measures for Public Libraries* (Zweizig and Rodger, 1982), which has since been revised and expanded in a second edition (Van House and others, 1987). Many of these measures have been modified for other library settings, for example, special libraries (McClure and Reifsnyder, 1984).

The Association of Research Libraries (ARL) sponsored the development of *Objective Performance Measures for Academic and Research Libraries* (Kantor, 1984), which offers standardized procedures for measuring

- materials availability: the chance that an expressed need for a specific document is met by the library
- materials accessibility: the degree to which various obstacles (defined in terms of effort and delay) affect the availability of a specific document.

The measures assess the "'quality' of library operations, [and] they all involve a mixture of the library activities with skills or promptness of the patrons" (p. 99).

In the United Kingdom, the Library Association and the Standing Conference of National and University Libraries (SCONUL) developed a set of measures of expenditures and library operations to determine the adequacy of university library funding and to help libraries negotiate for improved funding (Loveday 1988). Its list of about sixty measures focuses on relating expenditures to resources, internal operations, and quantity of services delivered.

The purpose of this brief review is to put the measures described in Part 2 into the context of earlier work. The discussion of each measure in Part 2 also reviews key works relevant to each measure.

This manual is not designed to introduce yet another set of measures so much as to build on, and select from, what has been done to present a single set of useful and easy measures. What has been missing is a set of basic output measures for academic and research libraries, emphasizing the user's experience, and documented so that any library can implement them without specialized training or help. This is the gap which the present manual is designed to fill.

The Approach of This Manual

There is no single, best way to do evaluation. A number of key choices must be made in designing an evaluation approach (Cameron and Whetten, 1983). The discussion below outlines the approach taken in this manual.

EFFECTIVENESS DEFINED

Effectiveness has been defined in many ways, including goal attainment, success in acquiring needed resources, satisfaction of key constituent groups' preferences, and internal health of the organization (Childers and Van House, 1989/90). This manual defines an effective library as one that achieves its goals. However, it must be acknowledged that academic and research libraries have many constituencies, often with conflicting needs and demands, which make it difficult for the library to develop a unified, prioritized set of goals. The emphasis here is on the quantity and quality of services provided to the library's major user groups.

THE PURPOSE OF JUDGING EFFECTIVENESS

The primary purpose of the measures in this manual is to assist internal decision-making and planning, including

- assessing current levels of library services
- comparing past, current, and desired levels of performance
- diagnosing particular problem areas or service
- monitoring progress toward specific objectives
- justifying internal resource allocations.

Secondarily, these measures provide a basis for describing levels of service and justifying expenditures to the library's external environment, including its parent organization, accrediting agencies, and the like.

These measures were not designed to be used to make comparisons across libraries. Chapter 2 discusses the limits to comparing these data across libraries. Local variations in measurement methods are necessary for local decision-making. And local variations in circumstances will affect the data. These same local variations may make the results noncomparable across libraries.

LEVEL OF ANALYSIS

Evaluation can take place at the level of the individual employee, the library subunit, the library, or the library system. The measures described in this manual assess performance at the level of the library subunit, generally the department or branch. In libraries with simple structures (e.g., a single facility with no branches), the level of analysis is the library.

SERVICES TO BE EVALUATED

Libraries provide a variety of services to a wide range of user groups. Although most academic and research libraries share a core set of services related to the provision of documents and information, each library defines the limits of its service areas and its relative priorities among them differently. Rarely does an organization operate equally well in all areas.

Because library services are multi-dimensional, so is library effectiveness: no single global measure of library effectiveness can summarize this multiplicity of services and clients (although there have been efforts to define one; see, e.g., Hamburg, 1974). A single measure assesses only one dimension of library performance. Multiple measures help to construct a more three-dimensional picture. So effectiveness must be measured by a set of measures covering the major library functions.

The library services addressed by the measures in Part 2 are:

- Overall user success, including success at various library activities, overall satisfaction, and ease of use
- Materials availability and use
- Facilities and equipment availability and use
- Information services.

EVALUATION PERSPECTIVE

If evaluation is an exercise of judgment, then conclusions will differ, depending on whose judgment is exercised. The assessment of effectiveness therefore depends in part on from whose perspective the evaluation is made.

The movement in librarianship has been toward judging library effectiveness from the perspective of the user (Powell, 1988), and this is the perspective adopted in this manual. The library's ultimate goal may be defined as meeting its users' information needs, which is best assessed from the users' perspective.

Users of libraries and other services are concerned with two basic issues: the outcome of the service transaction and the nature of the transaction (Klaus, 1985). Put simply, the user asks: "Did I get what I needed on this library visit? How easy was it?" Users are less concerned with how the library manages its operations than with whether their needs are met. The library is but a means toward this end.

Users' information-seeking process can be described as recognizing that they have information needs, determining how to meet those needs, then meeting them by using the library:

- Users come into the library with information needs
- They may use library resources to help determine how to meet their needs
- Users may be looking for information sources (books, journals, databases, etc.)—or information generally (information retrieved by either a librarian or the user)
- Users leave the library with their needs met, unmet, or potentially met. In the latter case, they may decide at a later time whether their needs were met (e.g., materials are requested). Or users leave with materials which they will review to determine how well the items meet their needs.

This is a simplified description of a complex process (Rohde, 1986; Dervin and Nilan, 1986). However, it forms the basis from which user-based output measures can be developed.

It must be acknowledged, however, that different user groups have different needs and priorities for the library. This complicates the evaluation process: Which user group's perspective is to be adopted in performing the evaluation? The library must balance differing and often conflicting needs among groups who may differ not only in their needs, but in their places in the library's environment and their roles in resource allocation within the library's parent organization. Furthermore, some groups relevant to library decision-making are not necessarily users at all, but other members of the library's parent organization—for example, faculty and administrators.

TYPES OF MEASURES

The various elements of the systems model of organizations depicted in Figure 1-3 form the basis for one categorization of measures. In theory, inputs, internal processes, outputs, and outcomes can all be measured, although in practice measurement gets more difficult as one moves through this progression. The emphasis in this manual is on measures of output.

Academic and research libraries currently keep and report a wide array of statistical data. Sources include ACRL (Molyneaux, 1989; Whiteley, 1985); the NCES HEGIS surveys (Center for Education Statistics, 1987), which have been replaced by the Integrated Postsecondary Education Data System (IPEDS); and the Association of Research Libraries (Daval and Feather, 1989). However, these measures are primarily inputs. The outputs reported are generally simple quantities of common services, such as circulation. These compilations are very useful, but the measures in this manual attempt to go beyond them.

Another way to classify measures is as objective or subjective. Objective measures are independent of any individual's assessment or perception. Subjective measures reflect people's judgments and perceptions.

The measures in this manual are a mix of objective and subjective. For example, the Materials Availability Survey asks respondents to report the numbers of items sought and found (objective) and their assessments of their success (subjective). Subjective measurement of library services and its relationship to objective measures has been insufficiently researched (see, e.g., D'Elia and Walsh, 1983). However, subjective measures of client perception of and satisfaction with library services are appropriate for at least four reasons:

- This manual stresses the user perspective on the library. One way to measure this is to ask the user directly.
- Clients or customers of service organizations, including libraries, are concerned with both service outputs and the nature of the service experience, the latter of which can only be assessed with subjective measures (Klaus, 1985; Mills, Chase, and Margulies, 1983).
- The definition of an information need and the assessment of the extent to which it is filled can ultimately be determined only by the library user (Dervin and Nilan, 1986).
- The user is the judge of the outcomes of library services (the effect on one's life or work, the uses to which the information is put). Outcomes

cannot be measured directly, but can be measured indirectly by user satisfaction.

| TIME FRAME | The measures in this manual offer a "snapshot" of performance, a static picture of library performance at a particular point in time. One-shot measurement provides useful information, but is limited. Most libraries look at their first measurement results and wonder: "Is this good? Are we improving?" Repeating the same measures periodically—generally every year or two—provides a more dynamic view of library performance over time. |

| EFFECTIVENESS REFERENT | Judging effectiveness ultimately requires that current performance be compared to what it should be. The basis for the comparison may be internal: against the library's performance at an earlier time or against the library's objectives.

Comparisons may, with care, be made externally—for example, among units in a library system, against "similar" libraries elsewhere, or against predetermined standards. Chapter 2 explains the difficulty with such comparisons. Slightly different measurement methods may result in significantly different measurement results. Data collected in two libraries at the same time may nevertheless differ because an exceptionally busy period in one library may be exceptionally quiet in the other.

Such comparisons must be carefully considered. They can only be made in the context of the parent institutions' missions, the libraries' missions and goals, and individual constraints and environmental factors.

Generally, output measures are best compared to internally produced criteria. Each library must decide the appropriate referent against which to compare its own performance. |

Conclusion

Carefully selected and intelligently used, output measures enable librarians to determine the degree to which objectives are accomplished, set priorities for resource allocation, justify services, and demonstrate the degree of library effectiveness to the library's parent organization and other agencies.

One key theme in this chapter is that "effectiveness" is a multi-dimensional construct which can be defined and measured in various ways. The measures and methods in Part 2 are based on the previous work in library measurement. They have been chosen to be valid and reliable while requiring a manageable level of effort for most academic and research libraries.

Chapter 2 addresses some general guidelines for measurement plus specific advice on the implementation and reporting of the measures in this manual.

MEASUREMENT

This chapter is about doing measurement. Specifically, it covers several topics necessary for understanding and doing good measurement and using the results in library management. It discusses:

- Criteria for good measures and measurement which underlie the instructions in this manual
- Choosing measures
- Managing the measurement effort, including sampling
- Presenting measurement results
- Using output measures data.

This chapter is aimed at the person(s) most directly responsible for implementing the measures in Part 2, but should also be read by anyone interested in understanding the measurement process and principles and the measurement results.

Success in implementing the measures in this manual requires:

- Support of management. The needed resources must be devoted to the measurement effort, and staff must believe that the data will be used.
- Understanding the principles underlying the measures. The instructions in Part 2 are designed to ensure good results, but this manual cannot give instructions to cover every possibility. To make decisions about measurement in your library you need to understand something about the principles underlying the methods in this manual.
- Attention to detail. The logistics of measurement are not complex, but appropriate procedures must be followed.

Criteria for Good Measurement

Good measures are valid, reliable, practical, and useful. The methods in Part 2 have been designed to maximize the measures' performance on these criteria. Changes to these methods should be made only with care, and with an understanding of how changes in methods affect the results.

Valid measures accurately reflect that which they are intended to measure. Circulation, for example, is a valid measure of the number of items charged out, but not a valid measure of total materials use, since it does not include in-library use. The detailed discussion of each measure in Part 2 explains what each is in fact measuring. Changing data collection methods may change what is measured. In interpreting and using the results, you need to consider what is and is not reflected in each measure.

A measure is *reliable* when the same thing is always counted the same way. Inconsistent data collection creates differences in results that may be due to differences in what is counted and how, not in library performance. The instructions in this manual are detailed to ensure reliability. However, this manual cannot anticipate every situation. And in some places we have identified alternative approaches from which you can choose. *For results to be consistent, the measurement methods must be consistent.*

To increase reliability:

- One person should be the final decision-maker on all measurement questions. When several units within the same library use the same measures, these decisions should still be made by one person (or a committee) to ensure consistency across units and across measures.
- All decisions should be documented and communicated to everyone who needs to know. A record of decisions will ensure consistency now and in the future, and will help you and your successors to understand the measurement results. (One approach is to keep a master copy of this manual in which you record all such decisions.)

Because of differences in data collection, output measures data are often not comparable across libraries, or even across units within the same library or library system. This is important to understand when making comparisons: *Incomparable data collection results in incomparable data.* The sheer number of measurement decisions that have to be made and the differences in how libraries and units operate make it very difficult to ensure comparability across units. The safest approach is to strive for comparability within a library or unit and to avoid making comparisons across libraries or units.

A *practical* measure is one for which data collection is relatively easy and straightforward. We have tried to make these measures as practical as possible.

Useful output measures provide information for decision-making. In deciding which measures to use, ask what actions or decisions will be helped by this information. Collecting data simply for its own sake is not only a waste of time and energy, the staff see that the data are not used and don't take data collection seriously.

Measurement decisions often require trade-offs among practicality, reliability, validity, and usefulness. Sometimes the most reliable and valid approach is difficult and complex. The most useful measure may be impractical. Each library has to judge the trade-offs it is willing to make, based on the uses to which the data will be put.

Choosing Measures

Decisions about which of the measures in Part 2 (outlined in Figure 1-2) to implement should be based on the relative costs and benefits of data collection, that is, the usefulness of the data compared to the effort required to collect them.

The usefulness of data depends on a number of factors:

- Which services are particularly important to your library?

- Does your library have problem areas about which you need more information?
- What decisions, changes, or opportunities do you anticipate in the near future?
- How can measurement data help?

The level of effort required to collect data varies among the measures. Those requiring a user survey (Materials Availability Survey, General Satisfaction Survey, Reference Satisfaction Survey, and Online Search Evaluation) require the highest level of effort.

Another concern is staff support or resistance. It is generally better to begin with measures that the staff do not find threatening, and that they perceive as being the most useful.

Managing the Measurement Effort

Measurement is not difficult. Nor does it require special training.

Data collection and analysis can be time-consuming. The methods in Part 2 are designed to be as easy as possible. Much of the data collection and analysis can be delegated to support staff or entry-level librarians, but they require the supervision of a professional, probably a mid-level manager or above.

One person should be responsible for the measurement effort. This person should have

- adequate commitment of time and energy to the measurement effort
- understanding of the library's services, organization, and operations, and insight into how library managers will use the data
- authority to marshal the resources to carry out the data collection and analysis
- attention to detail
- interest in the process and the results.

It helps if this person functions as a "measurement advocate," that is, takes the responsibility for showing other managers how the measurement data can be used and why measurement is important.

Preparing for Measurement

Adequate preparation is important to the success of data collection. Staff should be fully briefed on the purposes and methods of data collection. Those most closely involved in the library services being measured often have the best ideas about customizing the data collection and interpreting the results. Users will have questions about the data collection, especially for the measures most visible to them. Staff should be able to answer their questions.

With all the measures, a pretest—a small-scale dry run of data collection and analysis—will help you refine procedures and anticipate problems. The instructions in this manual are generic; you will need to fine-tune them for your circumstances. Because reliability requires that data be collected uniformly, you must be cautious about revising procedures once data collection has begun. A pretest allows revisions before data collection begins in earnest.

Sampling

A number of the measures in Part 2 utilize samples. Sampling consists of using a subset, or sample, of cases to represent a larger group or population. For example:

- The Materials Availability Survey collects data on a sample of user searches.
- The Reference Satisfaction Survey and Online Search Evaluation collect information on samples of reference transactions and online searches.
- For Facilities Use Rate and In-Library Materials Use, data may be collected during a sample period of time.
- Requested Materials Delay measures the time required to obtain a sample of requested items.

The discussion below addresses some of the basic principles of sampling that are helpful in understanding the instructions in Part 2. Some useful sources for more detail on sampling include Babbie (1989), Bookstein (1974), and Swisher and McClure (1984), or an introductory research methods text.

The basic principle is that a sample should be representative of the population as a whole. That is, all types of cases in the larger population should be represented in the sample in roughly the same proportions in which they occur in the larger population. The best way to ensure this is to draw a random sample; that is, every case (user, search, etc.) should have an equal chance of being selected.

The methods described in Part 2 are aimed at ensuring random samples. For example, insofar as possible every user entering the library during sample periods should be approached for the Materials Availability Survey. This prevents surveyors from avoiding people who seem busy, irritated, etc., which may bias the sample.

In projecting to the larger population from the sample, there is always some margin of possible error. This margin represents the possible difference between the estimate derived from the sample and the true value for the entire population.

It is important to realize that this margin, called sampling error, exists for two reasons:

1. The sample size required depends in part on the acceptable size of the margin. The larger the sample size, the smaller the margin. The sample sizes suggested in Part 2 are designed to give moderate margins. Smaller samples give larger margins, and vice versa.
2. Values derived from samples are *estimates. Small differences in measurement results across libraries or over time are generally not significant, but rather the result of the imprecision of these estimates.* The actual difference

attributable to sampling varies, but it is generally on the order of several percentage points (for measures reported as percentages).

This last point is very important. A difference of a few percentage points across libraries or over time is generally the result of sampling error, and does not necessarily reflect differences in library performance.

The instructions for Materials Availability include a table for estimating this margin because it is easy to do for this kind of measure. For most of the other measures, some knowledge of basic statistics is required to calculate the sampling error. We do not detail how to do this; but in interpreting the results for any measure based on a sample, keep in mind that there is always some sampling error or margin.

Readers who know how to calculate the confidence intervals for the means for the measures in this manual should do so. For the reader interested in learning, almost any introductory statistics text covers this.

The choice of sample size depends on how large a margin, or how much imprecision, is acceptable, not on the size of the larger population. The larger the sample the more precise the estimate. But the larger the sample the greater the effort required for data collection and analysis.

The choice of the appropriate sample size depends on other factors as well, which are beyond the scope of a manual intended for use in many different situations by readers with no training in statistics. Some colleges and universities have a campus statistical service that will advise on sample sizes. If yours does, it may be helpful to consult with the service before implementing the measures in Part 2, but it is not necessary.

The sample sizes recommended in Part 2 are rules of thumb, based on the experiences of libraries that pretested the measures in this manual.

Sample Periods

When collecting data during a limited or sample period of time, the period when data are collected will affect the results. For example, in academic libraries, materials are more likely to be on the shelf early in the term; but new students will have trouble finding their way around the library. As the term progresses, user success may increase (better-informed users) or decline (fewer items on the shelf). In some libraries, specific events (e.g., a large introductory class assigned a research paper) will affect the results.

The ideal would be to distribute data collection throughout the year. In most cases, however, this is impractical. IPEDS (the Integrated Postsecondary Education Data System) recommends that many data be collected during a "typical week." In most libraries there is no truly typical week, however; each is different.

One approach is to collect data during times that are relatively typical, knowing that no period is truly typical. Academic libraries should generally avoid periods very early in the term; when most classes are having midterms;

and during finals and term breaks. Research libraries should likewise avoid periods of especially heavy or light use, such as summer, when people may be on vacation or in the field; the Christmas holiday period; or times when many grant proposals are due.

Another approach is to deliberately pick a period for which you want data. For example, you may want to know what your Materials Availability Rate is during periods of heavy use, or what your Facilities Use is during final exams.

At any given time, different branches or departments of the same library may be subject to different influences. A science library's use may be affected by when students are in their labs; an undergraduate library is more affected by midterms than one that serves graduate students. Generally, a smaller or more specialized library will be subject to more variation due to its environment. In a larger or more diverse library, these influences are more likely to balance out.

In interpreting results, you must consider when the data were collected. Technically, your results are representative of only that period. If a measure is repeated periodically, do it at the same time of the term or year each time, so that results are roughly comparable.

Be cautious about collecting data on more than one measure at a time. Consider how the data collection efforts interact. For example, you may not want to do more than one user survey at a time; counting In-Library Materials Use could interfere with collecting data on Facilities Use; and so on.

Analyzing, Presenting, and Interpreting Data

Once data have been collected they must be summarized to make them understandable and useful. Appendixes A and B are comprehensive examples of reports on the general satisfaction and Materials Availability Surveys, respectively, that show some of the analyses that can be done.

Data can be analyzed manually or by computer. The instructions and reporting forms in Part 2 demonstrate the appropriate data analysis for each measure.

Computers can analyze large quantities of data with ease and reanalyze the data in different ways. Statistical software packages such as SPSSX, SPSS-PC, SAS, and ABSTAT are designed for just such applications. Statistical packages are the preferred software because they are designed specifically to analyze these kinds of data. If the library does not have PC software, many campuses have statistical software on a mainframe. If library staff do not know how to use statistical packages, you may be able to hire students or there may be a campus office that can help. (Appendixes A and B were created using SPSS-PC+.)

However, because sophisticated statistical tests are generally not needed, database management systems (DBMSs), such as dBase, or spreadsheet packages, such as Lotus 1-2-3, can also be used for many of these measures. DBMSs will allow more manipulation of the data; for example, you can pull

out all survey responses from faculty. Spreadsheet software is more limited, but can caculate totals and percentages, which are often all that is needed. (For a discussion of using microcomputers for library decision-making, see Hernon and Richardson, 1988.)

Chapter 3, "User Surveys," describes methods for analyzing user surveys by computer.

How the data are analyzed and reported depends to a large degree on how they will be used. It is useful to consider for each library:

- Who will see these data?
- How much detail do they need to understand them?
- What kinds of comparisons are useful?
- What questions will people be trying to answer with these data?
- What new and interesting information emerges from the data?

It helps for the person responsible for data analysis to first discuss the data informally with people who will be using them (unit managers, higher-level managers, etc.) to see what they want to know. The data presentation can then be tailored to these needs.

Many measures require that you calculate the *mean* or *average*. For many of the measures in Part 2, a tabulation form shows how to do this (e.g., Form 1-3 for the General Satisfaction Survey).

Be wary of averaging things that should not be averaged. For example, on user surveys it makes no sense to calculate an average for the question about purpose ("Today's visit was primarily in support of: teaching, research, etc."), although statistical software will happily do so for you. Instead, you should simply report the percent of users giving each answer.

When reporting percentages, it is important to report the number on which the percentage was based. Ten percent of 10 respondents is very different from 10 percent of 100 respondents.

Two questions, or variables, can be related to one another by cross-tabulation. This is particularly useful for relating the user or search characteristics on a user survey (Chapter 3) to the answers to other questions. Note that the percentages are the percentages of the members of each group who gave each answer, not vice versa. For example, on the Reference Satisfaction Survey (Form 14-1) you can cross-tabulate overall user satisfaction (question 5 on Form 14-1) with user status (question 6 on Figure 2-1). A useful discussion of cross-tabulation and table construction can be found in Babbie (1989).

Figures 2-1 and 2-2 are examples of two different approaches to cross-tabulation. Note that each has a title that explains exactly what it contains. In Figure 2-2:

- The base number for each percentage is reported. A reader could calculate the number in each cell using the base number and the percentages reported.
- The percentages add to 100 percent vertically; that is, the percents are column percents.
- The percentages are the percentage of each user group that gives each answer.

See Appendixes A and B for additional examples.

In analyzing subsets of data, such as looking at the differences in survey responses among user groups, however, caution is needed when some groups are relatively small. In Appendixes A and B, for example, relatively few faculty members were surveyed, no doubt because faculty are often a small proportion of the people entering an academic library. They may be heavier remote users (see Part 2) or may send research assistants. Their small numbers make their results of doubtful reliability.

Computers are a great help in presenting statistical results in an attractive and easy-to-understand format. The way that you present data will probably be determined (at least to some extent) by the software available to you. (The same results can be achieved manually, but computers make it much easier.)

Figure 2-1
Sample Analysis: Means by User Group

Mean fill rate (proportion of searches that are successful) by respondent purpose

	Mean	Cases
Course work	.5872	47
Teaching	.6250	4
Research	.6716	114
Current awareness	.5958	8
Mix of purposes	.6254	54
Other	.7821	13

Figure 2-2
Sample Analysis: Cross Tabulation
Purpose by User Group

Purpose		*Status*			
		Under-graduate	Graduate	Faculty	All Other
Course work	1	64.9%	16.0%	8.3%	2.2%
Teaching	2		3.1%		
Research	3		55.7%	66.7%	65.2%
Current awareness	4	3.9%	3.1%		2.2%
Mix of purposes	5	26.0%	19.8%	25.0%	13.0%
Other	6	5.2%	2.3%		17.4%
Column Total		77 100%	131 100%	12 100%	46 100%

Bar charts and pie charts present frequencies and percentages graphically. For example, Figure 2-3 is a bar chart showing the frequency with which people gave each possible answer to a question on the Reference Satisfaction Survey. Figure 2-4 is a pie chart showing the same data. More elaborate presentations can show more than one variable at a time; see, for example, Figure 2-5, which compares Facilities Use Rates for several facilities over three months.

Graphs or plots are most useful for presenting ordinal data, that is, data with some order to it. A common use for these data is to show changes over time. For example, Figure 2-6 presents circulation data over time. (When one axis of the graph is time, time should always be on the horizontal, or x, axis.)

A good source for further information on graphic presentations of data is Hernon (1989). Tufte (1983) contains an interesting discussion of graphical design and excellent, varied examples. The documentation for graphics software also generally presents useful explanations and examples.

Using the Results

Measurement is not an end in itself. For the data collection effort to be worthwhile, the data have to be used to improve library services. Output

Figure 2-3
Sample Bar Chart

Relevance of Information

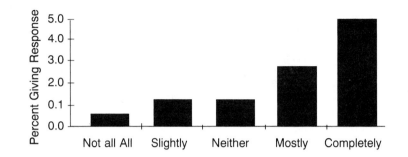

Figure 2-4
Sample Pie Chart

Relevance of Information

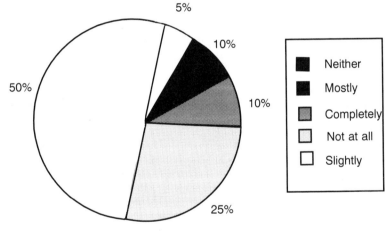

measurement results can form the basis for formal or informal library planning. The first step is to determine what the measurement results mean for *your* library, which is usually best done through discussions with all the staff involved. Service staff, in particular, often have valuable insights into the implications of the measurement results because of their closeness to the user.

It is helpful to disseminate the results widely among the staff. The benefits include:

- Giving staff feedback on their performance
- Demonstrating to staff that the data collection was meaningful, and not just another "make work" project. (Data collection is often more

Figure 2-5
Sample Bar Chart Comparing Several Variables

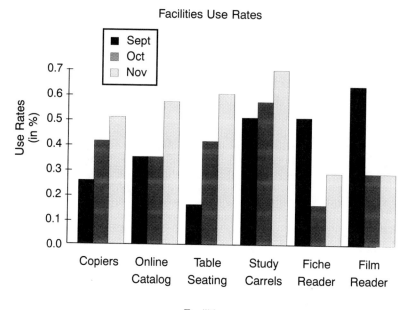

Facilities

Figure 2-6
Sample Graph

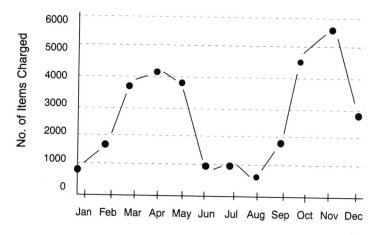

Month

accurate the second time around, after staff have seen the uses to which data will be put)
- Soliciting staff input in interpreting the results and planning actions based on them
- Fostering a results-orientation among the staff.

The data may reveal some problem areas that need further investigation. Staff may be able to speculate on the reasons for problem results, or further data collection may be needed. The sources for each measure cited in Part 2 can help suggest ways to collect more information.

Conclusion

This chapter has discussed some of the principles and logistics of measurement. A grasp of some of the reasons underlying the instructions in this manual will help the reader to understand why changes should be made only when necessary and with caution, why cross-library comparisons should be made only with extreme caution, and how to make some of the local decisions that are needed.

The next part of this manual details the specific measures, with data collection and analysis instructions for each.

USER SURVEYS

This chapter contains step-by-step instructions for conducting user surveys. It applies to:

- Materials Availability Survey
- General Satisfaction Survey
- Reference Satisfaction Survey
- Online Search Evaluation.

This chapter should be read in conjunction with the instructions for each of these surveys in Part 2. Sources for readers who wish to learn more about surveys include Babbie (1973 and 1989) and Martyn and Lancaster (1981).

Questionnaires

The user survey forms in this manual have been carefully designed to ask questions clearly and unambiguously. Designing comprehensive, clear questionnaires is difficult. These have been tested, revised, retested, and re-revised in a large number of libraries with a variety of users. *These questionnaires are not examples; they are to be used unchanged* (except for minor revisions to match them to a particular library, for example, changing the categories of user status as needed).

Users are very resistant to lengthy questionnaires. You will be tempted to ask a few more questions as long as you are doing a survey, but if too few users are willing to answer your questions, all your survey efforts will be wasted. It is better to do several short questionnaires at different times than one long questionnaire. These questionnaires are all one page or less, and *we strongly recommend that you not add questions.*

USER AND SEARCH CHARACTERISTICS

Questions about users and their searches are useful for analyzing the results for particular user groups or particular kinds of searches. Common to all the questionnaires in Part 2 are the following.

User Status. The appropriate user categories may vary across libraries. For academic libraries, these may be faculty, staff, graduate student, undergraduate, and other (e.g., for noncampus users). Some libraries may want to distinguish among undergraduate students by year or major; others may want details on noncampus users. In some institutions, faculty send research assistants to the library on their behalf; you may wish to include a category for them. Suggested wording:

If you came *on behalf of a faculty member* (e.g., you are a research assistant), check here:____

Categories should be unambiguous and mutually exclusive so that each user knows exactly which to check.

Academic Field. Another way to classify academic library users is by academic discipline. The categories that make sense depend on the library. For example, a branch library may be interested in specific departments while a general library may only need broad fields.

Respondents don't always know how their discipline is classified; many "other" answers can be recoded into the appropriate category.

Purpose of Visit. For what purpose will the respondent use this information or materials? The questionnaires in Part 2 list the most common purposes for academic libraries.

A given visit often has more than one purpose. You can either allow people to check more than one (which must then be allowed for in designing tabulation) or include as one of their choices "several purposes." The questionnaires in Part 2 take the latter approach. It gives less detail but is easier to tabulate.

Getting Ready

APPROVALS

You may need to clear the survey with your parent organization. Many universities require a review of any research that has people as its subjects, including library surveys. This human subjects review, as it is usually called, protects the welfare and confidentiality of your respondents. Contact the appropriate office on your campus for details—and remember that this may delay your survey by weeks or months.

PREPARING THE STAFF

The entire staff, including those not directly concerned with the survey, should be informed of the purpose of the survey and the procedures. Staff throughout the library are likely to be questioned by users ("Why are you asking all these questions?" "How do I answer this question?" "Where do I return the questionnaire?"). They should know the answers or to whom to refer questions.

Staff may feel threatened by any measurement, fearing that they individually are the targets of evaluation. This is particularly true of the Reference Satisfaction Survey. The more that they understand, the less threatened staff members will be.

Finally, staff may have practical suggestions about how to make the survey process run smoothly.

The best method for informing people is a staff meeting, preferably with the person in charge of data collection (see Chapter 2), so that they can ask questions. If a meeting is not feasible, memos, newsletters, etc., may be used.

PRETESTING

A pretest is a small-scale dry run. You *must* pretest survey procedures. Pretesting survey administration for perhaps an hour or so will help you refine procedures and discover possible problems early enough to resolve them. Pretesting can also provide an estimate of response rate and of how many questionnaires you can distribute per hour, which will help in scheduling data collection (see below).

If you have made changes to the questionnaires in this manual, you must also pretest these changes to be sure that they are clear and complete.

Deciding How Many Questionnaires to Distribute

The number of questionnaires distributed depends on the number of responses needed. Not every questionnaire handed out comes back, so you also need to estimate the proportion that will be returned.

Part 2 contains sample-size instructions for each survey. For the General Satisfaction Survey, we recommend 400 survey forms returned. For the Reference Satisfaction Survey and Online Search Evaluation, the numbers are considerably smaller. (see the discussion in Part 2.)

For the Materials Availability Survey (MAS), the calculation is more complicated since the target is the number of searches reported, not the number of forms returned. (See the discussion in Part 2.)

The response rate is the percent of people approached who returned completed and usable questionnaires:

$$\frac{\text{Response}}{\text{rate}} = \frac{\text{No. of completed questionnaires}}{\text{No. handed out + No. of refusals}}$$

The goal is a response rate of *at least* 50 percent. Less may mean that your respondents are not representative of your entire user group. For example, respondents may be particularly pleased with, or critical of, the library.

Our experience is that response rates in academic libraries run about 50 to 90 percent. The rates vary across surveys, with the Materials Availability Survey around 50 to 70 percent and the others about 70 to 90 percent. Rates also vary across libraries, with those serving primarily undergraduates at the lower end of these ranges. (People in the social sciences also seem particularly cooperative.)

If your pretest data are inadequate for estimate response rates, you may use the following default estimates:

General Satisfaction Survey   80 percent
Reference Satisfaction Survey   80 percent
Online Search Evaluation   50 percent
Materials Availability Survey   70 percent

Example for the General Satisfaction Survey: For a target of 400 responses, using the default estimates, distribute 500 questionnaires (400 = 80% of 500).

Scheduling

There is no ideal time to do a survey. In libraries with seasonal variations, like academic libraries, the results may vary depending on when data are collected. Chapter 2 discusses scheduling of data collection. For surveys, most libraries will want to pick a relatively typical time.

In reporting results, always include the date when the survey was done. In interpreting results, keep in mind possible influences on the results.

The days and hours during which questionnaires are distributed should be representative of all the days and hours that the library is open. The different times of day and days of the week should be represented roughly proportionately.

The number of hours during which questionnaires should be distributed depends on how busy the library is and how long it will take to distribute the target number. The pretest may help you to estimate this. Other local statistics (number of reference questions asked, number of people going through a turnstile, etc.) may also help.

It is generally best to collect data in an intense spurt over a week or so. The longer the time over which data are collected, the more likely that the same users will be surveyed again. *You do want repeat visitors to answer questionnaires again*, because you are measuring individual uses or visits, not users; but respondents may resist.

Administering the Survey

DISTRIBUTING
QUESTIONNAIRES

During sample periods, staff distributing the surveys should approach *every* person possible. The staff member tells each person, *briefly*, that the library is doing a survey to improve service and needs their cooperation. They should be polite but persuasive. (See Figures 3-1 and 3-2.)

Which users are to be approached depends on the survey (see instructions for each survey in Part 2). For example, the Reference Satisfaction Survey may be given only to people who asked reference questions, while the General Satisfaction Survey goes to all users. The Reference Satisfaction Survey and General User Survey are given to people as they leave the library or reference desk. The Materials Availability Survey is given to them as they arrive.

It is *very* important that as many of those surveyed as possible participate so that the results represent all kinds of users. The surveyors should not take "no" for an answer easily. They must be assertive but pleasant. (Keep this in mind in choosing staff, especially student library employees, for this task.) It helps to identify them as staff members—with a name tag, for example. People are more likely to cooperate if they know that the library is doing the survey.

In a very busy library, you may put more than one staff member at each entrance. The more people distributing questionnaires, the more they can distribute during a single time period, and the shorter the overall survey time.

Figure 3-1
Advice from a Surveyor

To achieve a reasonable return rate, the person passing out the surveys must be friendly, persuasive, persistent, and flexible. All kinds of people come into the library, most very busy and a few very rude, and you have only a short time to convince each one of them to fill out the form.

The opening line is crucial; it must be simple and short enough to be easily understood, but interesting enough to get the patrons' attention. For the Materials Availability Survey, the best line is something to the effect of "We'd like to know if you can find what you're looking for in this library." People will usually respond to this statement in some manner, or at least hesitate while they're thinking of past experiences. Of course, for the purposes of this survey, whether they can find it today is the important thing, but that's easy to explain once you've got their attention, and I've found that including that information in the opening line only confuses people.

I usually respond to their statements, which range from "I never find anything I want" to "I love this library!", with something like: "We need to know that; would you mind writing that in the space for comments, but filling out the survey just for your experience today?" For those people who merely hesitate, I usually add that we're trying to improve service in this branch, and we need to know how our users feel about our service.

If they still hesitate, I add whatever I judge will work with this patron. Some people want to know who is responsible for the survey (they want to be sure it's not just a student project); some are interested in the sampling technique; some want to discuss the concept of evaluating academic libraries; and some just want to know where the photocopy machine is. Whatever they want to know, I take the time to tell them; they become much more responsive to what I'm trying to accomplish.

As for convincing them of the importance of the survey, saying "This is really important" is *not* effective; I get this across more by my manner and my willingness to respond to their questions. And, I *always* tell them how much we appreciate their input, and thank them for filling out the form.

You do not need to cover all the entrances and exits, as long as there are no systematic differences among people using each door that will bias the survey (e.g., if the science offices and classrooms tend to be at one end of the campus and humanities at the other, so that each group is more likely to use one door to the library than another, you must cover both doors).

Most staff find that a two-hour shift is about the maximum for anyone to hand out questionnaires.

Do not simply leave questionnaires someplace with a sign asking users to complete them. The results will probably be skewed. Participants are likely to be either very pleased with the library or very displeased, and take the opportunity to tell you so.

Figure 3-2
Instructions for Surveyors

1. As far as possible, approach *every* person entering the library. Of course, sometimes you will be talking with one user while several others enter; but as soon as you are free approach the *next* person entering. *Do not* avoid people who look busy, important, irritated, flaky, etc. (Don't survey library staff members going about their jobs, however.)
2. It is important that *every* person approached cooperate. Be polite but persuasive. Explain to people that we need *their* response.
3. If possible, remind people on the way out to return questionnaires. Again, be polite but insistent.
4. Answer people's questions about the questionnaire as best you can, but be careful not to influence their answers (especially on the questions that ask for their opinions).
5. If people want to discuss the survey or the library, cooperate within limits; remember, you are there to dispense questionnaires. If they want to complain about or praise the library, encourage them to do so in writing on the questionnaire. Assure them that the powers-that-be will read the questionnaires so that is the best way to communicate their opinions.
6. Use Surveyor's Report [Figure 3-3] to report the number of questionnaires distributed: it's usually easiest to just count the number you begin with and the number left at the end of your shift.
7. Also report the number of people you approach who decline to take a questionnaire.

Count the number of questionnaires distributed and the number of people approached who refuse to cooperate (to compare to the number returned) to determine your response rate (see Figure 3-3).

Figure 3-3
"Surveyor's" Report

Name: _____

Library: _____

Survey: ____Materials Availability
           ____General Satisfaction
           ____Reference Satisfaction Survey

Date: _____   Time period: _____

1. NUMBER OF QUESTIONNAIRES DISTRIBUTED:

    Number of questionnaires you began with: _____
    Number of questionnaires left at end of time period: _____
OR:
    Total number of questionnaires distributed: _____

OR, if questionnaires have been numbered before distribution: _____
    ID # of first questionnaire handed out: _____
    ID # of last questionnaire handed out: _____

2. NUMBER OF PEOPLE WHO REFUSED TO TAKE A
   QUESTIONNAIRE: _____

3. NOTES (anything special you think we should know? Anything unusual that happened?) _____
_____
_____
_____

TURN THIS FORM IN AT THE END OF YOUR SHIFT WITH ANY REMAINING QUESTIONNAIRES.

COLLECTING
QUESTIONNAIRES

Place a box in an obvious place near the exit, clearly labeled "Return surveys here." The box should be sealed, with a slit in the top for questionnaires, to ensure respondents' anonymity. In a large library, it may help to distribute boxes in prominent locations around the library—for example, near the elevator on each floor for the Materials Availability and Reference Surveys.

If possible, staff at the door handing out questionnaires and at the circulation desk should remind people leaving to return their questionnaires. It is important to get back as many questionnaires as possible.

Analyzing Survey Forms

Questionnaires can be tabulated by hand or by computer. The worksheets and summary forms in Part 2 describe how to tabulate forms and summarize data for each measure. The summary forms suggest ways to present the final data, regardless of whether you use a computer.

The tabulation forms in Part 2 require that survey forms be numbered. If you can do this before distributing the forms, you know how many were given out and which ones came back. This is only practical for small surveys (such as Online Search Evaluation) or when tabulation is done by computer, since you won't want to put hundreds of forms in numerical order by hand to determine which are missing. Otherwise, number the forms as you tabulate them (a number stamping machine helps). This makes it possible to go back to a specific form if there is a question.

Before survey forms are tabulated, they should be reviewed for potential problems:

- Some questionnaires are hopelessly confused or incompletely answered and cannot be used. (These are subtracted from returned questionnaires in determining response rate.)
- Some questions are unanswered. *Never* infer what you think a user meant. If an answer cannot be tabulated as given, it is missing. (When using a computer, check to see how your software requires that missing values be coded.)
- "Other" answers can often be recoded to fit existing categories. For example, respondents may fill in their major rather than indicating an academic field.
- People will sometimes give multiple answers to a question that should have only one answer. These are treated as if the question were not answered at all.

On any survey, people make numerous comments about anything and everything. This is a significant side-benefit. You may want to circulate the survey forms to interested staff members or transcribe the comments and circulate this.

USING A
COMPUTER-BASED
STATISTICAL PACKAGE

To input your data, create a record for each returned survey form, with one variable for each question. Each variable can take on a set of values that correspond to the answers possible. For each variable or question, key the value that corresponds to the answer selected.

How you handle questions with missing or unusable answers depends on your software. Some software requires that "missing values," as these are called, be left blank. Other software requires a value be defined as "missing," which you then input for each question with a missing answer ("9" is a good choice). (Responses with missing answers should not be included in calculating averages and percentages. This is the purpose of "missing values" in statistical software.)

The following example shows the coding for the General Satisfaction Survey, Form 1-1. (Other questionnaires are handled in the same way.) For the General Satisfaction Survey, the suggested variables and values are as follows.

Question 1: Each part is a separate variable. Possible variable names:

- *BOOKS*
- *STUDIED*
- *CURLIT*
- *LITSRCH*
- *REF*
- *BROWSED*
- *RETBKS*
- *OTHER*

For each, key the number circled. "Did not do today" should be treated as "missing," so either key zero and define zero as missing or use whatever value your software uses for missing values. No answer on these questions is the same as "Did not do today." (This is the only time that you may infer an answer to an unanswered question.)

Question 2: EASE. Key the number circled; if no answer, it is "missing."

Question 3: SATIS. Key the number circled; if no answer, it is "missing."

Question 4: PURPOSE:

> *1 Course work*
> *2 Research*
> *3 Teaching*
> *4 Current awareness*
> *5 Mix*
> *6 Other*
> *If no answer, code missing*

Question 5: STATUS:

> *1 Undergraduate*
> *2 Graduate student*

Form 1-1
General Satisfaction Survey

PLEASE HELP US IMPROVE LIBRARY SERVICE BY
ANSWERING A FEW QUESTIONS.

1. What did you do in the library today? For each, circle the number that best reflects how successful you were.

	Successful?					
	Did not do today	Not at all				Completely
Looked for books or periodicals	0	1	2	3	4	5
Studied	0	1	2	3	4	5
Reviewed current literature	0	1	2	3	4	5
Did a literature search (manual or computer)	0	1	2	3	4	5
Asked a reference question	0	1	2	3	4	5
Browsed	0	1	2	3	4	5
Returned books	0	1	2	3	4	5
Other (what?)_____	0	1	2	3	4	5

2. How easy was the library to use today? *(Circle one)*:

          1   2   3   4   5
      Not at all easy   **Very easy**

      Why? _____

3. Overall, how satisfied are you with today's library visit? *(Circle one)*:

          1   2   3   4   5
      Not at all satisfied   **Very satisfied**

      Why? _____

4. Today's visit was primarily in support of *(Check one)*:
___1. Course work   ___3. Teaching   ___5. A mix of several purposes
___2. Research   ___4. Current awareness   ___6. Other:_____

5. You are *(Check one)*:
___1. Undergraduate   ___3. Faculty   ___5. Other staff
___2. Graduate student ___4. Research staff   ___6. Other (what?)_____

6. Your field *(Check one)*:
___1. Humanities ___2. Sciences ___3. Social Sciences ___4. Other (What?)_____

OTHER COMMENTS? Please use back of form.

3 Faculty
4 Research staff
5 Other staff
6 Other
If no answer, code missing

Question 6: FIELD:

1 Humanities
2 Sciences
3 Social Sciences
4 Other
If no answer, code missing

Any revisions of the form require that you revise these codes.

For the Materials Availability Survey, one variable should be the number of items found (number of "yes" answers), another the number of items not found. The total number of searches can be calculated by adding these together, so you don't need to key the total.

USING DATABASE MANAGEMENT SYSTEMS

Database management software (DBMS) such as dBase can also be used to analyze the data. The approach is similar to that with statistical software. A record is created for each survey form. A field is defined for each question on the form, and values assigned according to the answers given. In dBase, it is easy to calculate totals and averages for each field or question for all responses or for subsets such as user groups. It is more difficult to count the frequency with which each possible response is given: one must group on a field and then compute totals and averages.

It is more difficult to get a DBMS to do most analyses, and the reports are usually not as attractive and easy to read as those from a statistical package, but DBMSs give reasonably good results.

USING SPREADSHEET SOFTWARE

Spreadsheet software can be used to tabulate data. The keying of the data is somewhat cumbersome and not recommended if you have fewer than 100 questionnaires; in that case, it is faster to tabulate them by hand. Spreadsheets are limited in the analyses that they can perform; in particular, you cannot pull out a subset of responses (such as all faculty responses) to analyze separately.

Figure 3-4 shows how to set up the spreadsheet for tabulating the Reference Satisfaction Survey. (Spreadsheets for other surveys are similar.)

- Each row contains the data from one questionnaire.
- Column A contains the questionnaire number. Each of the following columns represents a possible answer to each question on the questionnaire. For example, question 1 on the Reference Satisfaction Survey has five possible answers. Columns B–F represent those answers. Column G is used for "no answer."

Figure 3-4
Spreadsheet Tabulation Example: Layout

	A	B	C	D	E	F	G	H	I	J	K	L	M	N	O	P	Q	R	S	T	U	V	W
1																							
2																							
3			Relevance					N		Amount				N		Complete				N		Help	
4		1	2	3	4	5	A	1	2	3	4	5	A	1	2	3	4	5	A	1	2	3	4
5																							
6																							
7																							
8																							
9																							
10																							
11																							
12																							
13																							
14																							
15																							
16																							
17																							
18																							
19																							
20																							

17-Oct-89 04:16 PM

- Key "1" in the cell which corresponds to the appropriate answer for the question.
- Total the columns after all the questionnaires are entered.

Figure 3-5 is a short example of a spreadsheet tabulation of fifty questionnaires. It shows the data for each questionnaire, and the totals at the bottom show the totals for each question. For the question on relevance of information, no one answered "1" or "2"; four people answered "3"; eight answered "4"; thirty-five answered "5"; and two did not answer the question.

Analyzing the Data

The same basic kinds of analyses are needed for each survey:

1. For each question, count the number of times each answer was given. Also count the number of times the question was left blank.
2. Calculate the *percentage* of 1's, 2's, etc., for each item.
   Exclude from percentages people who didn't answer the question.
3. Where possible, calculate the *average* score for the library. Again, exclude missing answers. For some questions an average makes no sense, for example, user status. Do not calculate an average for these questions.

Figure 3-5
Spreadsheet Tabulation Example: Data Entry

Reference Satisfaction Survey Spreadsheet Tabulation

#	Relevance 1	2	3	4	5	A	Amount 1	2	3	4	5	A	Complete 1	2	3	4	5	A	Help 1	2	3	4	5	A	Overall 1	2	3	4	5	A	Status U	G	F	R	S	O	A	Purpose C	A	R	T	O
1				1							1						1						1						1						1			1				
2				1							1						1						1					1	1						1						
3				1					1							1						1						1						1					1		
4				1						1							1					1						1					1					1			
5				1						1						1							1					1	1				1						1		
6				1							1						1						1						1				1								
7				1							1					1						1						1					1				1				
8				1						1							1					1						1						1			1				
9				1						1							1					1						1					1							1
10		1							1				1									1						1						1			1				
11			1							1				1								1						1					1				1				
12				1							1						1					1						1						1		1			1		
13				1							1					1			1						1			1						1							
14			1								1					1					1							1				1				1				
15				1							1				1					1					1				1					1							
16			1								1				1						1							1	1						1						
17			1								1				1						1							1				1				1				
18				1							1					1					1							1	1						1						
19			1								1					1					1							1							1					1
20				1							1					1					1							1					1			1				
21				1							1					1					1							1	1						1					
22				1							1					1					1							1							1					1
23				1							1					1					1							1				1								
24				1							1					1					1							1				1				1				
25				1							1					1					1							1				1				1				
26				1							1					1					1							1						1		1				
27			1								1					1					1							1	1						1					
28					1							1					1						1					1				1				1				
29				1							1					1					1							1	1						1					
30		1							1				1										1				1						1							
31			1								1					1					1						1						1							
32				1							1					1					1						1	1						1						
33				1							1					1					1						1	1						1						
34			1							1							1						1	1				1							1					
35		1								1						1					1					1		1							1					
36			1								1					1					1							1				1				1				
37		1							1							1					1							1	1 1						1					
38			1							1						1					1				1								1							
39				1							1					1					1						1	1											1	
40			1								1					1					1						1	1				1								
41				1							1					1					1						1		1			1								
42				1							1					1					1						1	1									1			
43				1							1					1					1						1			1					1				
44				1							1					1					1						1	1							1				
45				1							1					1					1						1	1										1	
46			1								1					1					1				1				1				1				
47				1							1					1					1						1	1						1				
48					1						1						1					1					1				1			1				
49				1							1						1					1					1					1			1				
50				1							1						1				1						1	1									1	
TL	0	0	4	8	35	2	0	0	5	13	30	2	0	0	5	12	31	2	0	0	1	16	31	2	1	0	3	13	31	2	17	16	1	1	3	9	3	11	4	18	1	8

You can also analyze the results separately for specific groups of users—for example, graduate students versus undergraduates or people using the library for research versus course work.

Appendixes A and B are comprehensive examples of analyses of the General Satisfaction Survey and Materials Availability Survey. Similar analyses can be performed on other surveys.

Be careful in interpreting the results for small groups. In Appendixes A and B, for example, the results for undergraduate and graduate students are probably valid; for the other groups, the numbers are so small that results are probably unreliable—that is, the addition of even one more respondent might change the results for that group.

The temptation might be to go back and survey only faculty for a while, or in some other way target an underrepresented group. This is fine *as long as those results are kept separate.* If faculty (for example) are a small proportion of total users, any effort to increase their numbers would result in their being represented disproportionately in the larger user sample. Simply adding them in with the other user groups would skew the results if, for example, faculty tend to look for more esoteric materials and so are less successful, on average, than the larger user group. The only way to include those additional faculty responses would be to weight them to reduce their impact on the total pool.

CONCLUSION

User surveys are not difficult if done carefully following the instructions in this manual. Respondents can provide valuable information about their library uses. A significant added benefit is that users are often pleased to have been asked. The survey demonstrates that the library cares about the users' opinions.

PART II
THE MEASURES

GENERAL

This part of the manual presents each of the measures individually, with detailed instructions. The discussion of each measure follows this format:

- *Definition* of the measure
- *Background,* including review of related literature. (This section may be skipped by the reader more interested in the how-to)
- *Data Collection,* including (as applicable):
    How to collect the data
    Forms
    Sample sizes and sampling methods
- *Data Analysis,* including (where necessary) tabulating the data and summarizing the results
- *Discussion* of what the results mean and how a library might go about improving its performance

---

1. General Satisfaction Survey

DEFINITION

Users' self-reports of:

- Success during this library visit on each of several possible library activities
- Ease of use of the library
- Overall satisfaction with today's library visit.

BACKGROUND

Most of the measures in this manual address specific services or facilities. In contrast, the General Satisfaction Survey is an attempt to obtain general information about the nature and outcomes of the user's library visit.

User studies are common in library evaluation (Powell, 1988). However, traditional library user studies have been criticized on a number of grounds (Swift, Will, and Bramer, 1979; Wilson, 1981; Streatfield, 1983; Rohde, 1986; Dervin and Nilan, 1986):

- In designing and evaluating libraries and information systems, evaluators impose system categories on people's behavior which may not fit users' experiences.

- The nature of users' needs, as well as how they express them, change over time, often during their search, as they learn more about their topic and the information available. User studies do not readily reflect this dynamic.
- Library and information system designers and evaluators see library use as an end in itself, whereas for users it is only a means toward meeting an information need. The information need, however, is more difficult to define and measure; so evaluation tends to be limited to the library use.

Researchers who have promoted a more user-centered approach have not yet been particularly successful in translating this into a feasible evaluation mechanism. The evaluation method developed by Dervin and Clark (1987), for example, is extremely time-intensive for both user and library.

However, users' evaluations of the success of their information searches are important to library evaluation. Users' satisfaction is determined only in part by the library's collection and its accessibility. But satisfaction helps to determine users' attitudes toward the library and probably their future information-searching behavior.

User assessments of services must be treated with caution, however. Research on libraries and other services has found that user characteristics significantly affect user evaluations; that is, different groups evaluate the same library differently (D'Elia and Walsh, 1983). It is not clear to what extent this reflects library performance versus user characteristics. Users' assessments, therefore, are best used in conjunction with other, objective data, that is, with the other measures in this manual.

User evaluations of a specific library transaction depend in part on what services were used on that visit and on the user's characteristics. The General Satisfaction Survey (Form 1-1), therefore, asks users to:

- List which of a variety of library activities they performed on this visit.
- Rate their success on each activity performed.
- Report their overall satisfaction with this visit.
- Rate how easy the library was to use.
- Describe the use(s) they will make of the information.
- Give basic demographic information about themselves.

DATA COLLECTION

Use the General Satisfaction Survey (Form 1-1). See instructions for User Survey (Chapter 3).

Form 1-1, question 1, lists the major uses that we have identified for some sample academic libraries. Consider whether this list is appropriate for your library. The demographic categories (question 5) may also need revision for your library.

In most cases you will need at least 100 completed forms; closer to 400 is preferable. Users are generally quite cooperative; response rates of 80 to 90 percent on the General Satisfaction Survey are common.

In some libraries it works best to give questionnaires to users as they leave. The questionnaire only takes a minute, and you avoid the danger of users losing them in the library or forgetting to fill them out. In some libraries, however, users on their way out of the library are reluctant to stop for any

Form 1-1S
General Satisfaction Survey

PLEASE HELP US IMPROVE LIBRARY SERVICE BY
ANSWERING A FEW QUESTIONS.

1. What did you do in the library today? For each, circle the number that best reflects how successful you were.

	Successful?					
	Did not do today	Not at all				Completely
Looked for books or periodicals	0	1	2	3	4	5
Studied	0	1	2	3	4	5
Reviewed current literature	0	1	2	3	4	5
Did a literature search (manual or computer)	0	1	2	3	4	5
Asked a reference question	0	1	2	3	4	5
Browsed	0	1	2	3	4	5
Returned books	0	1	2	3	4	5
Other (what?)_____	0	1	2	3	4	5

2. How easy was the library to use today? *(Circle one)*:
                    1   2   3   4   5
          Not at all easy   **Very easy**
          Why? _____

3. Overall, how satisfied are you with today's library visit? *(Circle one)*:
                    1   2   3   4   5
          Not at all satisfied   **Very satisfied**
          Why? _____

4. Today's visit was primarily in support of *(Check one)*:
   ___1. Course work   ___3. Teaching   ___5. A mix of several purposes
   ___2. Research   ___4. Current awareness ___6. Other:_____

5. You are *(Check one)*:
   ___1. Undergraduate   ___3. Faculty   ___5. Other staff
   ___2. Graduate student ___4. Research staff   ___6. Other (what?)_____

6. Your field *(Check one)*:
   ___1. Humanities ___2. Sciences ___3. Social Sciences ___4. Other (What?)_____

OTHER COMMENTS? Please use back of form.

reason, and you should give them questionnaires as they enter. Try both approaches during your pretest, and choose one.

DATA ANALYSIS

Summarize the number of times each possible answer was given to each question. Use Form 1-4 as a guide. User surveys may be tabulated manually or by computer, using a simple statistical package, database management system, or spreadsheet software. (See Chapter 3.)

Before tabulation, the questionnaires should be reviewed as described in Chapter 3, "User Surveys," for possible tabulation problems. If a questionnaire is hopelessly confused and cannot be tabulated, count it as "not usable." If an answer is unclear, or the respondent checks more than one answer to a question, do not infer what you think the user meant. If an answer cannot be tabulated as the user reported it, it is "missing" (the only exception is question 1). Many respondents don't bother circling the zeroes for all the activities that they didn't do. Treat no answer as "0."

A questionnaire that indicates that the user did not use the library—for example, someone reports that she or he came to look for someone, and was successful— should be treated as "not usable" because it does not represent an evaluation of the library.

The answers to the open-ended "why?" questions make for interesting reading. If you wish to tabulate them, read through enough questionnaires to define some recurring reasons; then count the number of times each type of reason is given.

Form 1-2 (General Satisfaction Survey Tabulation) can be used to tabulate the General Satisfaction Survey manually. (Any changes to Form 1-1 will require corresponding changes in Form 1-2). Record each questionnaire on a separate line on Form 1-2. The number of lines filled is the number of questionnaires tabulated.

You can also simply count for each question the number of times each answer is reported, without tabulating each questionnaire on a separate line as Form 1-2 does. The advantage to Form 1-2 is that you can go back and select subsets of questionnaires. For example, you can find all the responses from faculty and analyze those separately.

If the answers to some questions (but not all) are unclear or missing, draw a line through the space for tabulating that answer. You'll want to be able to come back and count the number of questions with missing answers. If an entire questionnaire is unusable, count it in the "not usable" box on Form 1-2, rather than putting it on a separate line.

Compute totals at the bottom of each copy of the tabulation form; then add the page totals from each copy of the form and record on Form 1-3, "General Satisfaction Survey Worksheet."

Code a few questionnaires on Form 1-2 and tabulate them on Form 1-3 before you do all the questionnaires—just to be sure that you understand what you are doing.

Whether you tabulate the surveys manually or by computer, you will do the same basic analyses. The computer does additional analyses with ease. Use Forms 1-2 through 1-4 for manual analysis. When using a computer, use Form 1-4 as a guide for the analyses to be produced. (Forms 1-2S through 1-4S are "worked examples" of Forms 1-2 through 1-4.)

Form 1-2S
General Satisfaction Survey
Tabulation

#	Looked for books 0	1	2	3	4	5	Studied 0	1	2	3	4	5	Reviewed current literature 0	1	2	3	4	5	Did a literature search 0	1	2	3	4	5
001		/					/						/						/					
002						/	/						/						/					
003	/								/					/					/					
004	/							/						/					/					
005						/	/						/						/					
006	/						/						/											/
007						/						/						/						/
008	/						/						/											/
009			/				/						/						/					
010	/						/			/			/						/					
011	/						/											/						/
012	/						/						/											/
013	/						/						/											/
014						/	/						/						/					
015			/							/						/						/		
016	/						/							/					/					
017	/						/						/						/					
018				/							/			/								/		
019	/						/								/									/
020	/						/									/			/					
Page Total	12	1	2	1	0	4	15	1	1	2	1	1	11	4	1	2	0	2	11	0	0	2	0	7

Not Usable: ~~HHt~~

1. For each question, count the *frequency* with which each value appears, that is, the number of 1's, 2's, etc., circled for each. Also count the number of times the question was left blank.
2. Calculate the *percentage* of 1's, 2's, etc. for each item.

For question 1, do *not* include in the base for percentages people who answered "Did not do today." You want only the percent of people who performed a given activity who were not at all successful, somewhat successful, etc.

Form 1-3S
General Satisfaction Survey Worksheet (pg. 1)

1. Number of questionnaires distributed: *432*
2. Number of questionnaires returned and usable: *381* (Enter on Form 1-4)
RESPONSE RATE: *88%* (Enter on Form 1-4)
    (Divide line 2 by line 1)

1. User Success in Specific Library Activities

Library Activity *Looked for Books*

(Fill in activity from Form 1-2 [e.g., Looked for Books or Periodicals], and compute totals from bottom of Form 1-2. One copy of this table should be completed for each library activity in question 1 of Form 1-1.)

(1) SUCCESS	(2) No.	(3) %	(4) No.	(5) %[1]	(6) (1)×(4)[2]
0 - Did not do today/No answer	*183*	*48%*			
1 - Not at all successful	*22*	*5.8*	*22*	*11.1*	*22*
2 - Mostly unsuccessful	*14*	*3.7*	*14*	*7.1*	*28*
3 - Neither	*47*	*12.3*	*47*	*23.7*	*141*
4 - Mostly successful	*42*	*11.0*	*42*	*21.2*	*168*
5 - Completely successful	*73*	*19.2*	*73*	*36.9*	*365*
Total	*381*	100%	*198*	100%	*724*

ercent of respondents who performed this activity. (Divide column 4 Total by column 2 Total) *52%*
o Form 1-4, line a).

verage (divide column 6 Total by column 4 Total): *3.66* (to Form 1-4, line b)

[1]Percent of total, column 4.

[2]Multiply the number in column 1 by number of responses in column 4.

Note: For the library activity "returned books," simply compute the % of respondents who reported that they returned books:

who returned books / total number of respondents

Enter percentage who returned books directly on Form 1-4.

    In some libraries you can use the percentage of people who gave answers other than "Did not do today" as the percent of people who performed each activity (Form 1-4). This requires that the people surveyed be representative of all users, which generally means that you surveyed people coming through all the entrances. If you do the survey in only part of the library—for example, in the reference room—you can only use this information to estimate the percent of reference room users who performed each activity.

    For other questions, exclude from percentages the people who didn't answer the question.

    For "returned books," just report the proportion of people who did it; don't bother with how successful they are. The reason for including this category is to give the people who came *simply* to return books a place to indicate this. The question could have been presented as a simple "yes/no" question (and this is how it is tabulated on Form 1-2), but if it were too easy,

Form 1-3s
General Satisfaction Survey Worksheet (pg. 2)

2. Ease of Use (compute totals from bottom of Form 1-2)

(1) Ease of Use	(2) Number	(3) Percent[1]	(4) (1) × (2)[2]
1 - Not at all easy	8	2.2%	8
2 - Not easy	17	4.7	34
3 - Neither	54	14.9	162
4 - Mostly easy	89	24.5	356
5 - Very easy	194	53.4	970
Total	362 [3]	100%	1530
No answer[4]	19		

Average (divide column 4 Total by column 2 Total): _4.0_

[1]Enter these percentages in Table 2, Form 1-4.
[2]Multiply the number in column 1 by number of responses in column 2.
[3]Enter this number in Table 2, Form 1-4.
[4]Do not use this number in calculating percentages.

3. Satisfaction with Library Visit (compute totals from bottom of Form 1-2)

(1) Satisfaction	(2) Number	(3) Percent[1]	(4) (1) × (2)[2]
1 - Not at all satisfied	18	4.9%	18
2 - Not satisfied	23	6.2	46
3 - Neither	67	18.2	201
4 - Mostly satisfied	99	26.8	396
5 - Very satisfied	161	43.6	805
Total	368 [3]	100%	1466
No answer[4]	13		

Average (divide column 4 Total by column 2 Total): **3.98**

[1]Enter these percentages in Table 3, Form 1-4.
[2]Multiply the number in column 1 by number of responses in column 2.
[3]Enter this number in Table 3, Form 1-4.
[4]Do not use this number in calculating percentages.

respondents might be tempted to say that they had come only to return books and avoid the other questions.

3. For questions 1 through 3, calculate the *average* score for the library. Again, exclude "missing" answers, including answers of "Did not do today" on question 1. (Note that for questions 4 through 6 an average would make no sense.)

Form 1-3S
General Satisfaction Survey Worksheet (pg. 3)

4. Purpose (compute totals from bottom of Form 1-2)

(1) Purpose	(2) Number	(3) Percent[1]
a. Course work	170	45.9
b. Research	105	28.4
c. Teaching	6	1.6
d. Current awareness	7	1.9
e. Mix of several purposes	48	13.0
f. Other	34	9.2
Total	370 [2]	100%
No answer[3]	11	

[1]Enter these percentages in Table 4, Form 1-4.
[2]Enter this number in Table 4, Form 1-4.
[3]Do not use this number in calculating percentages.

5. Status of Respondents (compute totals from bottom of Form 1-2)

(1) Status	(2) Number	(3) Percent[1]
a. Undergraduates	156	41.4
b. Graduate students	167	44.3
c. Faculty	15	4.0
d. Research staff	9	2.4
e. Other staff	9	2.4
f. Other	6	5.6
Total	377 [2]	100%
No answer[3]	4	

[1]Enter these percentages in Table 5, Form 1-4.
[2]Enter this number in Table 5, Form 1-4.
[3]Do not use this number in calculating percentages.

6. Field of Study (compute totals from bottom of Form 1-2)

(1) Field	(2) Number	(3) Percent[1]
a. Humanities	58	15.5
b. Sciences	64	17.2
c. Social sciences	222	59.5
d. Other	26	7.0
Total	370 [2]	100%
No answer[3]	11	

[1]Enter these percentages in Table 6, Form 1-4.
[2]Enter this number in Table 6, Form 1-4.
[3]Do not use this number in calculating percentages.

No. of Questionnaires Returned and Usable: _381_
Response rate: _88 %_

Form 1-4s
Summary of Results of General Satisfaction Survey (pg. 1)

Table 1. Summary of User Success Rates
(Enter percentages from column 5 of the tables in question 1, Form 1-3)

Activity / Success	a. Looked for books or periodicals	b. Studied	c. Reviewed current literature	d. Did literature search	e. Asked a reference question	f. Browsed	g. Returned books	h. Other
a. % of respondents who performed this	52%	45%	19.7%	31.2%	20.5%	18.8%	20%.	N/A
Of users who performed this activity, % who were (from Form 1-3, column 5):								
1 - Not at all successful	11.1 %	4.7%	8%	4.2%	3.8%	5.8%		
2 - Mostly unsuccessful	7.1	7.0	12.0	5.9	1.3	10.1		
3 - Neither success nor unsuccessful	23.7	16.3	26.7	21.0	11.5	26.1		
4 - Mostly successful	21.2	23.8	29.3	30.3	16.7	23.2		
5 - Completely successful	36.9	48.3	24.0	38.7	66.7	34.8		
b. Average rating (from Form 1-3)	3.66	4.04	3.5	3.9	4.4	3.7		

DISCUSSION

Users come to the library for many purposes, with differing expectations. Only the user can say how successful and how easy this visit was, in his or her opinion.

This survey asks users about this particular visit because this approach is generally more accurate than asking general questions about how successful people usually are. People's memories of previous visits and "usual" experiences are often biased by exceptional occurrences, both good and bad.

The list of activities in question 1 can be either library- or user-oriented. This list is user-oriented; it contains the major uses for which a person comes to the library—not all the activities a person could perform while in the library. Every library user must be able to find in question 1 something that they did. The reason for including "returned books," for example, is not to find out how successful people were, but because some visits are for only this reason.

Users' assessments of the success of their visits and satisfaction with the library depend on many factors, including:

- Outcome of this visit
- Their expectations of the library
- Library's resources
- Library staff's behavior
- User's ability and efforts
- Importance to user of each of library services and facilities used.

Form 1-4s
Summary of Results of General Satisfaction Survey (pg. 2)

Table 2. Ease of Use

(Enter the percentages from question 2, column 3, Form 1-3. Enter the average from the bottom of the table in question 2, Form 1-3.)

Not at all easy	Not easy	Neither easy nor difficult	Mostly easy	Very easy	Total	Average rating
2.2%	4.7%	14.9%	24.5%	53.4%	100%	4.0

# of responses _362_ (Total, column 2, Form 1-3)

Table 3. User Satisfaction with Library

(Enter the percentages from question 3, column 3, Form 1-3. Enter the average from the bottom of the table on question 3, Form 1-3.)

Not at all satisfied	Mostly dissatisfied	Neither satisfied nor dissatisfied	Mostly satisfied	Very satisfied	Total	Average
4.9%	6.2%	18.2%	26.8%	43.6%	100%	3.98

# of responses _368_ (Total, column 2, Form 1-3)

Table 4. Purpose (Enter the percentages from question 4, Form 1-3)

Course work	Research	Teaching	Current awareness	Mix of purpose	Other	Total
45.9%	28.4%	1.6%	1.9%	13.0%	9.2%	100%

# of responses _370_ (Total, column 2, Form 1-3)

Table 5. Status of Respondents (Enter the percentages from question 5, Form 1-3)

Undergraduates	Graduate students	Faculty	Research staff	Other staff	Other	Total
41.4%	44.3%	4%	2.4%	2.4%	5.6%	100%

# of responses _377_ (Total, column 2, Form 1-3)

Table 6. Field of Study (Enter the percentages from question 6, Form 1-3)

Humanities	Sciences	Social sciences	Other	Total
15.5%	17.2%	59.5%	7.0%	100%

# of responses _370_ (Total, column 2, Form 1-3)

Some users will report success when a librarian might not, and vice versa. Some users will be unrealistically critical of the library; some overly forgiving. However, users' self-reports of success provide valuable information about how they view library experiences.

The causes of user lack of success and dissatisfaction are many. A library whose survey results indicate problems should consider possible causes and solutions. Talking with users and the staff who serve them will often turn up at least some of the major problem areas.

In most libraries, use is largely self-service; so the library must be easy to use. Some libraries are inherently more difficult to use than others. But low ratings on ease of use may suggest a need for improvement. Better signs, more accessible staff, more flyers or posters on how to use the library, and bibliographic instruction are all possible remedies. The open-ended comments will help to pinpoint areas where improvements are needed.

FURTHER SUGGESTIONS

Cross-tabulate questions 1 through 3 with questions 4 through 6 to determine how success in various activities, ease of use, and overall satisfaction varies by purpose, status, and/or field. (See Chapter 2 for an example of cross-tabulation.)

Look for patterns by time of day or day of week. (This requires coding questionnaires by time of day or day of week.)

MATERIALS AVAILABILITY AND USE

A major library function is the provision of materials. In this manual, this is measured in several ways:

- Use of library materials
    - circulation of materials outside the library
    - in-library use of materials
- Materials availability: likelihood that users will immediately find materials that they need
- Requested materials delay: time elapse for user to receive requested materials

How well the library meets its users' needs for materials depends on a number of factors, including how well the collection is matched to users' needs, the library's efforts to make the collection accessible, and the users' efforts and ability to locate the materials needed.

Of course, materials-use measures do not necessarily reflect the entire value of the collection. In research libraries, evaluation of the collection must incorporate its other purposes besides current use (e.g., its archival value). Materials availability and use measures are useful, however, in evaluating the library's ability to meet its users' needs for documents.

2. Circulation

DEFINITION

The annual total number of items charged out for use, usually (although not always) outside the library, includes initial charges, renewals, and general collection and reserves (which may be separated). This definition is the same as that for the Integrated Postsecondary Education Data System, 1988 (IPEDS). Use your IPEDS data, if available.

DATA COLLECTION

Most libraries count circulation on an ongoing basis. It is important to ensure that all units in the library are using a consistent definition. Frequently the circulation count is considered a workload figure, and items charged to internal library units (i.e., reserves, bindery, mending, cataloging) are included in the statistics. Although this is a useful number, it may overestimate use by patrons.

DATA ANALYSIS	Simply sum your ongoing circulation counts for an annual total.

DISCUSSION	Circulation is a basic measure of the extent of use of libraries' collections. Without considering In-Library Materials Use, Circulation may substantially underestimate the use of a collection.

FURTHER SUGGESTIONS	Calculate Circulation per capita by dividing Circulation by the number of people in your primary user group. How you count users and whom you include will vary across libraries. For academic libraries, one possibility is students plus faculty plus research staff. For nonacademic research libraries, this total may be researchers in the institution.
	Automated circulation systems may provide detailed information about circulation by user group or by segments of the collection. Count the Circulation for each class of users; or calculate the Circulations per person in each class of users.
	Calculate Circulation for specific parts of the collection (e.g., by classification or shelving location or type of material).
	Calculate Circulation per volume held, for the entire collection, or for parts of it.
	Divide Circulation by hours open to get circulation per hour.
	Record Circulation by day of week, time of day, or week of academic term to find periods of heaviest use.

3. In-Library Materials Use

DEFINITION	Total number of items used in the library but not charged out.

BACKGROUND	Libraries have traditionally counted circulation of materials. However, simply counting circulation underestimates the total use of the library. Recently, libraries have also begun to count in-library use of materials in several ways:

- By asking users not to reshelve materials used in the library (Kent and others, 1979; Van House and others, 1987)
- By observing users' behavior and counting their uses (Wenger and Childress, 1977)
- By asking users how many materials they used during their visit (Rubin, 1986)
- By placing questionnaires in selected materials, asking users who find them to complete them (Taylor, 1976/77).

Different methods give different results (Rubin, 1986), and it is not clear which is the most accurate. Differences may be due to a number of factors, including users' inability to remember how many materials they used, users' failure to cooperate with obtrusive methods, or differences in the definition of "use" (is a title consulted at the shelf, then deemed irrelevant, used or not?). The table count is certainly the easiest.

Metz and Litchfield (1988) and McGrath (1971) found fairly high correlations between circulation and in-house use in large libraries for the entire collection. They concluded that circulation and in-house use are similar but not identical. The accuracy of correlating circulation and in-house use will depend upon circulation patterns and which materials circulate. For example, in a library where the majority of the collection does not circulate, the correlation may not be valid.

DATA COLLECTION

In academic libraries, patterns of materials use change during the term. The most accurate count of In-Library Materials Use is obtained by counting all materials used in the library at all times or during an entire term. If users are routinely asked not to reshelve items, the staff simply needs to count all materials gathered for reshelving.

However, if counting all In-Library Uses at all times is not feasible, you can count during a sample period. Choose one or two (preferably two) relatively typical weeks (see Chapter 2). It is best to do the survey in a short, concentrated period; users will be confused if you ask them not to reshelve in the morning, but to reshelve in the afternoon, then not to reshelve the next day. It's helpful if you can also count your Circulation for this same period (see "Data Analysis," below).

How often during the day you collect and count materials depends on levels of use in your library. Presumably, the materials will be there when you come to collect and count. However, consider how often you should count and collect materials to keep user work areas clear and the collection in reasonably good order. Also, high-use materials left on user work tables may be used more than once between counts if you collect materials infrequently.

During a sample period (or continuously), ask users not to reshelve materials. Count all materials collected. Some libraries routinely ask users not to reshelve materials; in this case, the only change is that during the sample period you count the materials you pick up.

If your users generally reshelve materials, place signs prominently around the library:

LIBRARY SURVEY IN PROGRESS. PLEASE DO NOT RESHELVE MATERIALS

You may want to designate places for users to place materials to be reshelved, or simply pick up materials wherever people have used them.

In deciding whether to count a specific kind of use as an In-Library Use, your concern is that all uses be counted once and only once; each use should be counted as *either* a circulation *or* an in-house use. For example, reserve materials that are charged are *not* counted here, because they are counted as Circulations. Materials that are paged for users but not charged should be counted as In-Library Uses.

Do not simply count all materials shelved (which would include charged materials counted under Circulation). Count materials picked up for reshelving, not materials currently being used, since they will be counted when the patron is through with them. Inevitably, some users will reshelve materials, regardless of what you do; but you want to minimize this.

Some uses are almost impossible to count, for example, browsing unbound periodicals or using periodical indexes. Do the best that you can, but remember no measure is perfect.

During busy times staff may forget to count In-Library Use. Placing statistics sheets (see Form 3-1; 3-1S is an example) in convenient places (such as near sorting shelves) may help remind staff to count.

DATA ANALYSIS

If you count In-Library Materials Use on an ongoing basis, simply sum this for your annual total.

Form 3-1 s
In-Library Materials Use

Library *Undergraduate*
Date *November 16*

Use one tally sheet for each day. At designated times, collect and count the materials left for reshelving. Enter the time at the top of the form.

Area or Type of Material	Hour															Totals
	9 AM	10	11	12	1	2	3	4	5	6	7	8	9	10	11	
1st floor		133		118		213		199		179			136			978
2nd floor		86		151		175		242		171			193			1018
3rd floor		159		124		199		241		137			99			959
4th floor		15		125		156		145		191			31			663
Micro-forms		0		15		23		37		8			19			102
Totals		393		533		766		864		686			478			

If you count In-Library Materials Use for an entire term, you can estimate your annual total (including vacation periods) by dividing In-Library Materials Use by Circulation during that same term, then multiplying that percentage by your annual circulation.

Example: If In-Library Use for one semester is 70,000, circulation for the same semester is 50,000, and annual circulation is 120,000:

$$70,000/50,000 = 1.4$$
$$1.4 \times 120,000 = 168,000$$

annual In-Library Uses

If you count use only during a sample week or two, it is most accurate to simply report your use during that period, without extrapolating to an annual total, since patterns of In-Library Use may change during the year and the academic term.

If you wish to project to an annual total, however, divide In-Library Materials Use by Circulation during that period to calculate In-Library Materials Use as a percentage of Circulation. Then apply this percentage to your Total Annual Circulation to derive Annual In-Library Materials Use.

Example: If In-Library Use for a typical two-week period is 10,500, Circulation for the same period is 14,555, and annual circulation is 350,000:

$$10,500/14,555 = .72$$
$$.72 \times 350,000 = 252,000$$
annual In-Library Uses

Relating In-Library Materials Use to Circulation assumes that In-Library Materials Use is a constant proportion of circulation, which may not always be the case. (You can test this assumption by counting In-Library Materials Use at various times in the academic term and comparing it to Circulation.) However, these methods result in annual estimates of acceptable accuracy.

DISCUSSION

In some libraries, In-Library Materials Use is a large proportion of the total use of the collection. Circulation figures may understate the collection's use.

In-Library Materials Use is often coupled with use of the library for research and studying (rather than simply retrieving materials and leaving). Increasing In-Library Materials Use may suggest a greater need for study space, copy machines, or reshelving staff. High In-Library Materials Use may be accompanied by large numbers of Reference Transactions, if people are using the library for research. High In-Library Use, coupled with slow reshelving, may contribute to user failure to find materials (see "Materials Availability," below).

FURTHER SUGGESTIONS

Many of the "Further Suggestions" for Circulation also apply to In-Library Materials Use:

Calculate In-Library Materials Use per capita by dividing In-Library Materials Use by the number of people in your primary user group.

Calculate In-Library Materials Use for specific parts of the collection (e.g., by classification, shelving location, or type of material).

Calculate In-Library Materials Use per volume held, for the entire collection, or for parts of the collection.

Divide In-Library Materials Use by hours open to get In-Library Materials Use per hour.

Record In-Library Materials Use by day of week, time of day, or week of academic term to find periods of heaviest use.

4. Total Materials Use

DEFINITION	Total number of uses of library materials of all types.
DATA COLLECTION	See "Circulation, Data Collection" and "In-Library Materials Use, Data Collection," above.
DATA ANALYSIS	Add Circulation to In-Library Materials Use for comparable periods, for the entire year (if you have annual data for both), or for a sample period (if you measure In-Library Materials Use only during a sample period).
DISCUSSION	In many libraries where In-Library Materials Use is large, Circulation underestimates use of the collection. Total Materials Use is a more valid reflection of collection use.
FURTHER SUGGESTIONS	Many of the "Further Suggestions" for Circulation and In-Library Materials Use also apply to Total Materials Use:

> Calculate Total Materials Use per capita by dividing Total Materials Use by the number of people in your primary user group.
>
> Calculate Total Materials Use for specific parts of the collection (e.g., by classification or shelving location).
>
> Calculate Total Materials Use per volume held, for the entire collection or for parts of it.
>
> Divide Total Materials Use by hours open to get Total Materials Use per hour.
>
> Record Total Materials Use by day of week, time of day, or week of academic term to find periods of heaviest use.

5. Materials Availability

DEFINITION	The proportion of actual user searches for library materials that is successful at the time of the user's visit. This includes all kinds and formats of materials.

BACKGROUND

A major approach to evaluating a library's document provision is to measure how often users find that what they are looking for is immediately available.

Mansbridge (1986) reviews over forty availability studies published over fifty years. These studies consist of checking a sample of titles (monographs and/or serials) against the library's collection to determine what proportion is owned and available. A key methodological decision is the source of the items to be tested. The majority of the studies reviewed by Mansbridge use titles for which users were actually looking (e.g., Van House and others, 1987). Other sources include:

- The shelflist (e.g., De Prospo and others, 1973)
- Abstracts, indexes, and bibliographies (e.g., De Prospo and others, 1973)
- Items cited in the publications of the libraries' clients (Orr and others, 1968a)
- Lists generated by subject experts.

Sources other than actual user requests are much easier to deal with than actual requests and more convenient for the library and its users. However, they are of doubtful validity in that they never perfectly represent all the kinds of materials for which all kinds of users are looking. Furthermore, researcher-generated samples rarely reflect the actual distribution of requests across titles, with a few titles accounting for many multiple demands. Using actual requests, however, is difficult and obtrusive; that is, it may affect the users' behavior.

Zweizig and Rodger (1982), Van House and others (1987), and Kantor (1984) describe methods that use actual requests. The result is the percent of user searches that were successful. Another way to say this is that it is the probability that a search will be successful.

Kantor presents a method for diagnosing the causes of search failures by having the staff immediately follow up user searches to determine the status of items not found. This method yields rich information, but is labor-intensive.

The method presented below asks users to list the items for which they searched and their success. The questionnaire only asks for known items, monographs, serials, or other formats, not subject searches. It does not matter whether the user came to the library seeking a specific item, or with a general subject need and identified titles using the library's catalogs and indexes. The question is: What is users' success rate in finding materials on the shelf? The measure does not seek to diagnose the causes of failures; for this, readers are referred to Kantor (1984).

DATA COLLECTION

Use Materials Availability Survey (MAS), Form 5-1. (See instructions for User Surveys in Chapter 3.) You may need to change the user status categories to suit your library.

Determine sample size (see below) and schedule (see Chapter 3), and give a questionnaire to every user entering the particular area during the sample

Form 5-1
Materials Availability Survey

DID YOU FIND IT?

PLEASE HELP US IMPROVE SERVICE by telling us whether you found the library materials you looked for today. Use this form as scratch paper while you look in the catalog and on the shelf.

Your status (check one):

_____1. Undergraduate   _____4. Research staff
_____2. Graduate student   _____5. Other staff
_____3. Faculty   _____6. Other (what?) _____

If you were NOT looking for library materials today, please check here _____ and stop. THANK YOU!

Author/Title/Journal/etc. (abbreviations are fine)	Call #	Found on shelf? CIRCLE
_____		Yes No
_____		Yes No
_____		Yes No
_____		Yes No
_____		Yes No

OVERALL, how <u>successful</u> were you at finding materials today?

        1   2   3   4   5
     Not at all   Completely successful

What will you use these materials for? Primarily:

_____1. Course work   _____4. Current awareness
_____2. Research   _____5. A mix of several purposes
_____3. Teaching   _____6. Other: _____

MORE ITEMS? COMMENTS? Use the back of this form. THANK YOU!

PLEASE DROP IN BOX AT EXIT AS YOU LEAVE.

period. If a large proportion of users are not searching for materials but are coming to study, for example, you can survey only people who are searching for materials. Surveyors ask each person, "Are you going to be looking for library materials [or books or periodicals] today?", and give questionnaires only to those who answer "Yes." Note that you cannot use the survey results to estimate the proportion of library users searching for materials unless you survey *all* users or keep careful count of the number of people approached who say that they are not searching for materials. (If surveyors ask these people for demographic information—e.g., academic field and status—you can compare searchers and nonsearchers.)

The needed sample size refers to the number of *searches* needed, not the number of users surveyed. Many users aren't looking for materials, and report no searches. Others look for more than one item, and report more than one search per questionnaire.

Table 5-1 shows how sample size relates to sampling error (see Chapter 2) for dichotomous measures such as Materials Availability (where materials are or are not available). The sampling error, or margin, depends on the results as well as the sample size. Choosing the sample size requires a rough estimate of your results, which may come from a pretest, previous experience, other libraries' experiences, or a wild guess. If all else fails, use a worst-case approach: Given the margin you are willing to live with, what is the largest sample size that you might need?

This is the way to read Table 5-1:

- If a library's Materials Availability Rate (the proportion of searches that are successful) is about 50 percent and it has 400 materials searches, its true rate is within 5 percentage points of the survey results. Its Materials Availability Rate is 50 percent plus or minus 5 percent, or between 45 and 55 percent.
- For a Materials Availability Rate of about 90 percent, with 400 materials searches, the true value is 90 percent plus or minus 3 percent, or between 87 and 93 percent.
- If a library expects its Materials Availability Rate to be about 60 percent, and it can live with a margin of 5 percentage points in either direction, then it needs a sample of about 384 questionnaires. To reduce the margin to plus or minus 2.5 percentage points, it needs 1,600 searches reported.

Thus, reducing the margin requires increasing the sample size considerably.

The 95% confidence level in Table 5-1 means that your estimate is 95 percent likely to fall within this range; that is, there is a small (5 percent) chance that the true value falls outside the range of the interval calculated.

This confidence interval (as it is called) around each estimate is impor-

Table 5-1

Number of Observations Needed to Estimate Percentages
(95% confidence level)

Percent breakdown	+2.5%	+3%	+3.5%	+4%	+4.5%	+5%	+6%
10–90	576	400	294	225	178	144	100
20–80	1024	711	522	400	316	256	178
30–70	1344	933	685	525	414	336	233
40–60	1536	1067	784	600	474	384	267
50–50	1600	1111	876	625	494	400	278

tant because it means that *small changes in measurement results based on samples may be due only to sampling error.*

> *Example:* One year a library has a Materials Availability Rate of 60 percent plus or minus 5 percent, or 55 to 65 percent. The next year it is 63 percent plus or minus 5 percent, or 58 to 68 percent. The Materials Availability Rate may not be different—we say that there is no significant difference—from one year to the next because both years overlap at 58 to 65 percent.

An added consideration in choosing sample size is how many questionnaires, reporting how many searches, you can collect within a reasonable period of time. A small library, where many users are doing things other than looking for materials, may find it difficult to collect reports on more than 100 or so searches.

Translating the number of searches reported to the number of questionnaires to hand out depends on the expected response rate (see Chapter 3, "User Surveys"), the expected proportion of questionnaire reporting searches, and the average number of searches per questionnaire. If necessary, you can use the following default estimates, derived from several academic libraries' experiences:

Response rate	70%
Questionnaires reporting materials searches	50%
Average number of searches per questionnaire reporting materials searches	2.0

Using these figures to determine the number of questionnaires to distribute is best explained with an example:

> *Example:* A library sets its target at 400 searches (using Table 5-1):
> 400 searches require 200 questionnaires reporting searches (2 searches per questionnaire that reports searches).
> 200 questionnaires reporting searches require 400 questionnaires returned (200 is 50% of 400).
> 400 returns require 570 questionnaires distributed (400 is 70% of 570). Therefore, this library must distribute 570 questionnaires.

The same results can be achieved by using the formula X = S/PQR, or X = S divided by PQR, where

X = number of questionnaires needed
R = response rate (estimated)
Q = % of questionnaires expected to report searches
P = expected average number of searches per questionnaire
S = target number of searches

The example works out to:

$$570 = \frac{400}{(2)\,(.7)\,(.5)}$$

If the library in this example found 570 MAS questionnaires overwhelming, it would go back to Table 5-1 to determine whether it would be satisfied with a larger margin and thus a smaller sample size.

A library may repeat the Materials Availability Survey at different times during the year or the term. Most libraries, however, will only want to do it once every year or two. If you repeat the survey annually or biennially, it is best to do it at the same time of year or term if possible.

DATA ANALYSIS

Form 5-2 may be used to tabulate surveys. Form 5-2S is a worked example. The Materials Availability Rate consists of dividing the number of successful searches by the total number of searches. Form 5-3 is a worksheet, and Form 5-4 a summary. Forms 5-3S and 5-4S are completed examples.

Because the Materials Availability Rate is an estimate, with potentially a wide margin of sampling error, once you have calculated your Materials Availability Rate you must use Table 5-1 to calculate this margin. Find the Materials Availability Rate along the left side (e.g., a rate of 60% is a 60-40 breakdown; a rate of 40% is the same). Then, on that line, find the approximate number of *searches*. At the head of the column is the value for your margin. Enter this margin on Form 5-3, line 13, and Form 5-4, line 1a.

For example, on Form 5-4S, the Materials Availability Rate is 64% for 282 searches. In Table 5-1, we look at the 40-60 percent breakdown line (rounding the 64%) for the number closest to 282. The figure in the last column is 267, which is close to 282. The number for "accuracy," at the top of the last column, is 6%. We enter 6% on line 13 of Form 5-3.

This tells us that our Materials Availability Rate of 64% is not very precise; it could actually be as small as 58% or as large as 70%.

Form 5-2 is for tabulating MAS questionnaires manually. Tabulation is also easy with a simple computer statistical or spreadsheet package, which also allows for more manipulation of the data. (See Chapter 3.)

If a questionnaire is hopelessly confused and cannot be tabulated, it is not usable. Count unusable questionnaires to deduct from your total of "questionnaires returned and usable" in calculating your response rate (on Form 5-2, put a mark in the box "Cannot Tab"). If the answers to some questions are unclear or missing, *do not infer* what you think the user meant; if an answer cannot be tabulated as the user reported it, it is "missing."

Inevitably, some users will list what is clearly a subject (e.g., "books on local architecture"); do not count such responses.

To use Form 5-2, tabulate each questionnaire on a separate line. By counting the number of copies of Form 5-2 and the number of lines filled you have a count of the number of questionnaires tabulated.

You can simply count the numbers of successes and failures, and the number of times each answer was given for each of the other questions. The line-by-line approach of Form 5-2 allows you to go back and analyze subsets of questionnaires; for example, you can find all the graduate students.

When a question is not answered, draw a line through the spaces for that question on Form 5-2. This makes it easy to go back and count "no answers."

These are the line-by-line directions for tabulating questionnaires when you use Form 5-2:

- ID number: key.
- Status: Mark the appropriate column on Form 5-2.

Form 5-2 S
Materials Availability Survey
Tabulation

#	Status 1	2	3	4	5	6	Not Looking	# Found	# Not Found	Success 1	2	3	4	5	Uses 1	2	3	4	5	6
001	/						/													
002		/						3	2			/			/					
003	/							2	0				/		/					
004				/			/													
005	/						/													
006		/						3	1			/						/		
007	/							0	4	/										
008	/							1	0				/		/					
009	/						/													
010		/						3	0				/			/				
011		/						2	1			/					/			
012			/					3	1	/									/	
013	/						/													
014	/						/													
015		/					/													
016	/							1	1			/			/					
017	/							2	0				/						/	
018	/						/													
019	/							2	0				/		/					
020		/						5	4			/				/				
021		/					/													
022	/							1	0				/		/					
023			/					2	0							/				
024	/							1	0				/		/					
025		/					/													
026	/							1	0				/							
027		/						4	2			/			/					
028		/						2	1			/						/		
029				/				1	0											/
030	/							1	0				/							
Page total	16	10	1	1	1	1	10	38	17	1	1	4	3	9	7	4	1	1	3	1

Cannot tab: ＨＨ /

Library_____   Date_____

- Not looking: Put a mark in this column if user has checked this space. There should be no other information entered on Form 5-2 if this space is checked.
- Found: Count the number of "yes" circles. Be sure to check the back of each questionnaire for additional items.
- Not found: Enter the number of "no's." Check the back.

Form 5-3 s
Materials Availability Survey Worksheet

1 - Number of questionnaires distributed	600
2 - Number of refusals	19
3 - Total (1) + (2)	619
4 - Number of questionnaires returned and usable	368
5 - Response rate (Divide line 4 by line 3)	59%
6 - Number of respondents not searching for material (Total from "not looking" column, all copies of Form 5-2)	125
7 - Number of questionnaires reporting searches (Subtract line 6 from line 4)	243
8 - Number of items found (Total from "found" column, all copies of Form 5-2)	315
9 - Number of items not found (Total from "not found" column, all copies of Form 5-2)	177
10 - Total searches (Add lines 8 and 9)	492
11 - Average number of searches per person looking for materials (Divide line 10 by line 7)	2.0
12 - **Materials Availability Rate** (Divide line 8 by line 10 and enter on Form 5-4, line 1a)	64%
13 - Margin: plus or minus (from Table 5-1, using # from line 10; see instructions; enter on Form 5-1, line 1b)	6%

(If the user listed items but did not mark yes or no, do not count. If there are items listed but no yes or no circled, draw a line through the "found" and "not found" spaces.)

- Success: Mark one of lines 1 through 4, depending on whether the user checked the first line ("not at all successful"), second ("mostly unsuccessful"), etc.
- Purpose: Mark one of lines 1 through 6, depending on which line the user checked. If the user has marked more than one space, that is the equivalent of "a mix of several purposes," and should be coded 5. Mark that space on the user's survey in red to indicate that the coder made that change.

Compute totals at the bottom of each copy of Form 5-2, then add and record on Form 5-3. Also total for each question the number of "no answers."

Note that item 2 on Form 5-4 requires that you analyze all respondents, then (optionally) just those who reported searches. To do the second part, go back through all copies of Form 5-2 to tabulate only those who did *not* check "not looking." Alternatively, when tabulating questionnaires, you can tabulate *only* those that were looking for materials, and not bother with the rest. In that case, fill in only the "searchers" part of Form 5-4, item 2, and leave the "all respondents" part blank. For answers to common questions about tabulating the Materials Availability Survey, see Figure 5-1.

No. of Questionnaires Returned and Usable: _368_

Response rate:_____

Date of Survey: _10/89_

Form 5-4s
Materials Availability Survey Summary (pg. 1)

1. Materials Availability Rate (from Form 5-3, line 12) (a)_64%_   + or − (b)_6%_
(from Form 5-3, line 13)

2 Status of respondents
   (Totals from "status" column, all copies of Form 5-2)

Status	All respondents		Searchers[1] [optional]	
	Number	Percent	Number	Percent
Undergraduates	80	28.6		
Graduate students	138	49.3		
Faculty	13	4.6	N/A	
Research staff	8	2.9		
Other staff	8	2.9		
Other	33	11.8		
Total	280	100%		100%
No answer	2			

[1]Respondents who were searching for materials. "Optional": see instructions in text. From Form 5-2, count only respondents who did not check "not looking."

3. Overall user materials search success rate
   (Totals from "success" columns, all copies of Form 5-2)

(1) Success	(2) Number	(3) Percent of line 6	(4) (1) × (2)[1]
1. Not at all successful	60	21%	60
2. Mostly unsuccessful	10	3.5%	20
3. Neither	5	1.8%	15
4. Mostly succesful	25	8.9%	100
5. Very successful	180	64%	900
6. Total	280	100%	1095
No answer[2]	2		

Average (divide column 4 Total by column 2 Total): _3.9_

[1]Multiply the number in column 1 by the number of responses in column 2.
[2]Do not use this number in calculating percentages.

4. Uses of materials
   (Totals from "uses" columns, all copies of Form 5-2)

Uses of Material	Number	Percent
1. Course work	73	27.2%
2. Research	111	41.4
3. Teaching	5	1.9
4. Current awareness	8	3.0
5. Mix of several purposes	56	20.9
6. Other	15	5.3
Total	268	100%
No answer	14	

Figure 5-1
Some Common Questions about Tabulating the Materials Availability Survey

A user didn't indicate whether she found something, so I figured she must have found it. Was this the right thing to do?

Don't infer! You don't know *whether the user found it or not.*

Many users gave incomplete bibliographic information about the items they looked for. Do we count those?

Yes. We ask users to list each item so that they will report on specific searches and not simply estimate how many things they looked for and how many they found. Although it helps show gaps in the collection, we don't really need any bibliographic information from them.

Some users say something like, "Looked for 4 items and found 3." Do we count these?

Yes.

What about people who say, "Looked for various things and found them." Do we count them?

No.

We found completed questionnaires lying around the reading room. Can we count them?

Yes.

What about people coming in to pick up materials that are being held for them? This means that they came in twice for that item, once unsuccessfully and then again, later, successfully. Do they count?

Yes. Don't drive yourselves crazy splitting hairs on what to count and how. People who come in on a survey day, who don't find what they want and place a hold, are counted as "unsuccessful." Someone coming in on a survey day to pick up something on hold counts as a successful search.

Lots of our use are students coming in to get reserve readings, sample exams, and the like. Do we count them?

Decide whether you want to include them, and be consistent. Requests for reserve readings, sample exams, etc. are materials searches, too. If you do a large volume of these requests and feel that they will skew your results, count them separately. Add a column to the questionnaire asking whether each item was a class reserve, etc., then tabulate them separately.

What about people who call ahead to have us hold materials for them?

Again, don't drive yourselves crazy with details. This is only important in a library where this is a large volume of total activity.

What about our document delivery service? Users phone, fax, or e-mail requests and we deliver materials to their offices.

You should include your document delivery service (DDS) in your materials availability survey. This is generally easy. Have the DDS keep track of the number of filled and unfilled requests, which many do anyway. Calculate a separate materials availability rate for the DDS rather than try to fold it into your survey results. You should probably calculate a Requested Materials Delay (see p, 71) for the DDS, too.

You can also go back through the copies of Form 5-2 to pull out other groups of responses. For example, you can analyze all the responses from faculty to determine their Materials Availability Rate.

| DISCUSSION | This measure reflects users' success in finding specific items in the library. A user is successful when the library owns the item, it is on the shelf, and the user finds it. Note that this is not the proportion of *users* who are successful, since one user may report more than one search. This is the proportion of *items* sought that are found. |

This measure reflects users' success in finding specific items in the library. A user is successful when the library owns the item, it is on the shelf, and the user finds it. Note that this is not the proportion of *users* who are successful, since one user may report more than one search. This is the proportion of *items* sought that are found.

Users who are doing subject searches are asked to list the items that they identify (such as from the catalog). The measure reflects the probability that users will find items in the collection and on the shelf, regardless of whether they identify the item before or after entering the library. An important limitation of this measure is that it only reflects the success of users who come to the library and respond to the survey form. Remote online catalog access can substantially impact Materials Availability Rates since many unsuccessful catalog searches will not be recorded. (Presumably, many successful searchers will subsequently come to the library or order the item).

A high Materials Availability Rate means that users often find the specific items that they are looking for immediately.

Searches may be unsuccessful due to either library or user failure: the item may be not owned, not cataloged properly, or not on the shelf; or the item may have been there but the user failed to find it. This measure does not distinguish among causes of failures.

Each library must decide whether its Materials Availability Rate is acceptable. Some users look for things outside the library's scope, and others fail to find things that are exactly where they belong; however, no library can supply all its users' needs immediately. A large noncirculating collection or restricted loan periods will generally increase the Materials Availability Rate, although this may dissatisfy some users because materials cannot be borrowed.

If your Materials Availability Rate is unacceptable, here are some possible solutions:

- Staff often have ideas about the causes of user failure; so try acting on some of these perceived problems, and repeat the Materials Availability Survey at some later date to see if things have improved.
- Make staff more available to help users who fail to find what they are looking for.
- Talk informally with users about causes of failure, to see if you can identify needed changes.
- Do the Materials Availability Survey as an interview, rather than self-administered questionnaire, for a few hours and ask users about their experiences.
- Kantor (1984) presents a method for a Materials Availability Survey in which the staff follow up on user searches to determine the cause of failure. This provides useful information, but requires a higher level of effort than the approach described here. (Kantor's approach may be more appropriate for *some* libraries than the method presented here.)

FURTHER SUGGESTIONS	Consider a short online survey asking users of online catalogs with remote access whether they found what they were looking for in the catalog and, if so, whether they intend to pick up the item at the library or order it from a document delivery service. (Unfortunately, it is much more difficult to program a survey into an online catalog than to hand out questionnaires.)

Read through the completed questionnaires for a sense of the kinds of searches that fail.

Tally the categories of searches that fail—by general subject, call number, format, or whatever seems useful.

Tally the searches for each group separately and calculate a Materials Availability Rate for faculty, students, etc. Note that results for small groups will be very rough estimates (refer to Table 5-1).

Tally separate Materials Availability Rates for different purposes, using the answers to the "purpose" question. Some libraries place a higher priority on supporting instruction than research, for example, and would like to know how well they are doing in different areas. |

6. Requested Materials Delay

DEFINITION	Length of time users must wait to receive (or have available) requested material that is not owned or on the shelf. This may be computed as the proportion of materials requested that are available within x number of days, or as median number of days required to receive requested materials.
BACKGROUND	When materials are not immediately available, either because they are not on the shelf or not owned, most libraries offer users the option of requesting them. Libraries greatly differ in their approaches to availability. Some prefer to have as much as possible available, others stress efficient procurement or retrieval. Some libraries rely on acquiring items only as they are needed. Lancaster (1977) and Buckland (1975) discuss various approaches for evaluating document retrieval services.

Orr and others (1968b) measured the delay in acquiring materials drawn at random from a pool of recently cited items. Unlike Orr's measure, Requested Materials Delay is concerned with actual user requests rather than requests generated by the researchers. It does not diagnose causes of failure; for this, see Kantor (1984). |
| DATA COLLECTION | Decide which requested materials service you would like to evaluate. Possibilities include circulation recalls, off-site storage retrieval, special material acquisition (such as theses and technical reports), library document delivery service, or interlibrary loan. |

A library with a volume of 100 or more requests in one category per month (whatever category(s) you wish to track) can collect data on all the requests initiated during a sample month (see Chapter 2). In libraries with fewer than 100 requests per month, it is most accurate to keep an ongoing count for all requests.

Each service (circulation, interlibrary loan, etc.) should be responsible for keeping its own log. During the sample period (or on an ongoing basis), code each request in such a way that, when the requested material arrives, you can update the log. Staff record the date the patron makes the request, the request number, and an identifying piece of information (e.g., patron name or title of the requested item) on the log. Multiple requests by the same patron for different materials should receive its own number. (See Requested Materials Log, Forms 6-1 and 6-1S.)

Decide whether you wish to record the date the material becomes available for the user, the date the user is notified, or the date the user receives the material. It is undoubtedly easier to record the date material is available to the patron, but this method will not pick up added delays created by the notification method (e.g., slow mail service). The date the patron receives the material may add the variable of the time after notification that it takes the patron to pick up the material. The date the user is notified is the most useful date. However, with mail notification it may be difficult to ascertain this accurately.

Although different services within an institution may choose to use different dates (e.g., circulation recall may choose to use the date the patron is notified; document delivery may choose the date the material is delivered to the patron), each service must be consistent with its choice. It is not possible to compare services if different dates are used.

Some services may wish to determine the number of hours, rather than days, required to fill a request. In this case, record both the date and time.

Note: Maintaining this information on a log may not be practical for some libraries. It is possible to keep all of the required information on the request slip and fill in the log at a later time. However, marking which requests are in a sample could indicate to staff that these requests should be expedited.

DATA ANALYSIS

Calculate the delay time by using the log sheet (Form 6-1; Form 6-1S is an example) to determine the difference between the date in column C (date request made) and the date in columns D (date request arrives) or E (date patron notified), or both. Count the actual days (including days the library was closed) between the dates. Do not count the date of the request, but count the date the request arrives (column D) or the date the patron is notified (column E).

> *Example:* If a patron requests a recall on an item September 28 and the item is available October 3, the delay time would be 5 days.

It is possible to calculate either the percentage of requests available within various time periods or the median delay, or both.

Use Form 6-2 (Form 6-2S is an example) to calculate the percent of requests available within various time periods, and those canceled (e.g., user cancels). For an interlibrary loan, 7, 14, 21, 30 days and even more may be

Form 6-1s
Requested Material Log

A # of Request	B Patron Name or Title of Request	C Date Request Made	D Date Request Arrives	E Date Patron Notified	F Delay Time (C–D)	G Delay Time (C–E)
1	P. Royen	9-18	9-20	9-20	2	2
2	D. Harder	9-18	9-21	9-21	3	3
3	L. Casher	9-20	9-25	9-25	5	5
4	M. Sequin	9-21	9-25	9-25	4	4
5	B. Warren	10-2	10-6	10-8	4	6
6	B. Warren	10-2	10-6	10-8	4	6
7	J. Patton	10-2	10-6	10-8	4	6
8	J. Patton	10-5	10-10	10-10	5	5
9	K. Carpenter	10-5	10-9	10-10	4	5
10	R. Park	10-10	10-13	10-15	3	5
11	R. Park	10-10	10-16	10-16	6	6
12	R. Freeman	10-10	10-16	10-16	6	6
13	F. Dewey	10-10	10-16	10-16	6	6
14	W. Davis	10-16	10-23	10-23	7	7
15	C. Muslow	10-20	10-24	10-24	4	4
16	J. Pierce	10-21	10-24	10-24	3	3
17	J. Pierce	10-23	10-24	10-24	1	1
18	K. Alcorn	10-23	10-24	10-24	1	1
19	J. Field	10-24	10-30	10-30	6	6
20	C. Hoffman	10-25	10-30	10-30	5	5

appropriate. For other types of delivery systems, less than 1 day, 1 day, 2 days, or more than 2 days may be appropriate.

You may wish to determine the median delay for each type of request (see Form 6-3). (The median is the value at which half the cases are above the median and half below.) The median is useful where a few very large (or very small) values may skew the mean. With requested materials, items that are requested but don't come for years (if at all) will inflate the mean, so the median is used instead.

Form 6-2S
Requested Materials Delay

Delay	Number	Percentage
1 day	HHT HHT III 13	14 %
2-3 days	HHT HHT HHT II 17	18 %
4-5 days	HHT HHT HHT HHT IIII 24	25 %
6-7 days	HHT HHT HHT HHT HHT II 27	28 %
8 or more days	HHT HHT IIII 14	15 %
Canceled	0	0
Total	95	100%

To determine the median by using Form 6-3:

- List, in increasing order, the times of delay from Form 6-1.
- Tally the number of requests with each delay time.
- Sum the cumulative total of requests. When the cumulative total is equal to or more than half of the total number of requests, you have reached the median delay time. (See Form 6-3S for a worked example.)

DISCUSSION

Libraries cannot provide all the materials their users want at all times. This measure indicates how quickly a library can fill requests for material not available on the shelf. Each service will have to decide whether its wait for

Form 6-3 s
Requested Materials Delay
Median Determination Worksheet

Delay	# of Requests	Cumulative Total	
1 day	13	13	
2 days	7	20	
3 days	10	30	
4 days	12	42	
5 days	12	54	←median
6 days	14	68	
7 days	13	81	
8 or more	14	95	95/2 = 47.5

requested materials is acceptable. Libraries with unacceptably long waits may want to pursue further analysis to identify the cause of delays. For one approach, see Kantor (1984).

Remedies to delay problems depend on the service involved. Some possibilities are:

- Streamline ordering and processing of material.
- Increase frequencies of deliveries (this may include mail or intralibrary deliveries).

- Divide your workflow and create a "rush" processing flow, or document expediters for the most critical portion of the requests.
- Examine alternative sources or methods of procurement (fax?).

Finally, consider the items being retrieved. Should they be owned by the library? Are more copies or shorter loan periods needed?

FURTHER SUGGESTIONS

Calculate separate delay times for different sources of materials (e.g., using traditional interlibrary loan sources versus information brokers).

Count the total number of materials requested and calculate this total as a percentage of the total circulation for the same time period.

Review requests that have long delay times: Can they be categorized by type of material, subject, source, etc.?

FACILITIES AND LIBRARY USES

The measures in this section have to do primarily with the use of the library's physical facilities: numbers of people entering the library building, the availability of specific facilities, and the use of library services. However, in recent years technology has made it increasingly possible for users to substitute electronic communications media for a trip to the library. Library uses that once required the user's presence do so no longer. Yet these users are still "using" the library. "Remote" use of library services often enhances the quality of service by making the library more convenient, even making the library accessible to people for whom it was inaccessible before.

7. Attendance

DEFINITION

Number of user visits to the library—that is, the number of people entering the library, including people attending activities, meetings, and those requiring no staff services. This definition is consistent with IPEDS, but period of data collection may differ. (See "Data Collection," below.)

For a different approach to counting the number of people using the library, see measure 12, "Building Use," below.

DATA COLLECTION

Two approaches are possible:

1. *Door counter.* Many library turnstiles and security systems count the number of people passing through. (Many libraries with turnstiles don't use this function and don't realize that they have it.) You can reset the counter periodically, or record its reading periodically and subtract.

The door counter will, of course, count staff as well as users. No correction for this is possible. If people pass through the library door counter on their way elsewhere (e.g., to classrooms or offices), this count will overstate library use. If people hold the security gate open for one another, it will undercount the number of people passing through. But it is a useful approximation, and much easier than the sampling method.

Door counters can be rented for a sample period. This may be the easiest solution for a library with no counter, though door counters can be purchased fairly inexpensively.

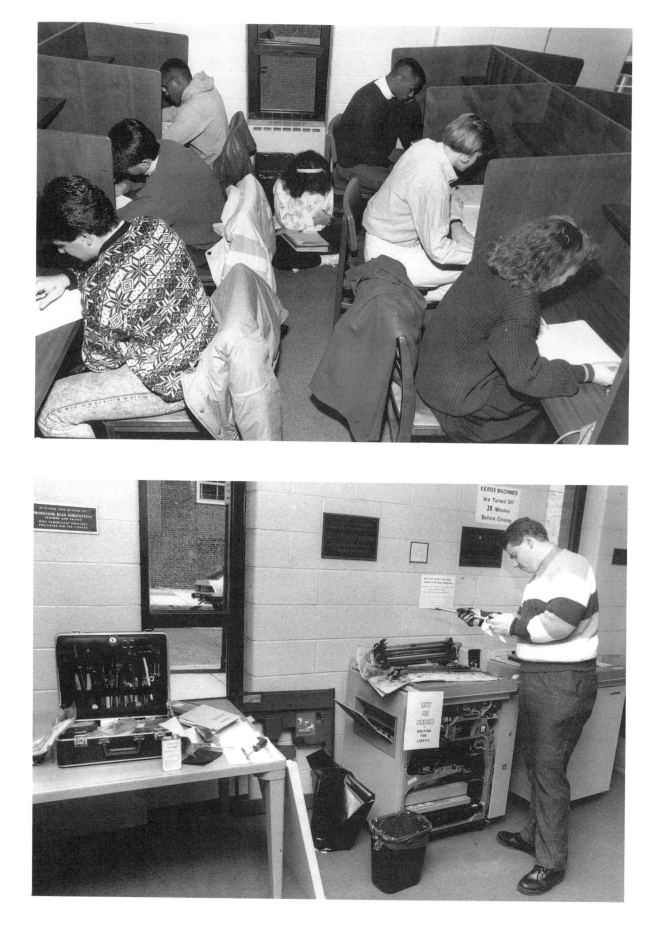

2. *Sample.* In a library without a door counter, a staff member takes the place of the door counter (in effect) and counts people who enter the library during sample periods of time.

If you wish, in some cases you may be able to avoid counting staff members, people coming in to use the rest rooms, etc. In many cases this will be difficult or impossible, so we do not recommend that you try to make such corrections. If the data are to be compared to those collected via door counter—another branch or department, for example, or the same library at another time—you do *not* want to correct for staff, because then your data will be noncomparable.

The period during which you collect data will determine your results. The simplest solution is to pick a reasonably representative period (e.g., a relatively busy time), but (in academic libraries) not during midterms or finals or periods of other unusual activity (see Chapter 2).

We recommend that you collect data all day, every day, for one or (preferably) two weeks.

DATA ANALYSIS

In a library with a door counter, simply total the number of people passing through the counter during the year.

In a library that counts attendance during a sample period of time, data analysis is more difficult. ANALYSIS of data from academic libraries with door counters shows that attendance in the library varies considerably during the period of the term and is not related to easily counted activities (such as Circulation). This means that there is no easy way to project a week or two's worth of data on attendance to an entire academic year.

We recommend, instead, that the data be reported for the period for which it is collected. That is, report that during the week(s) of _____ , X number of people passed through your doors. When repeating this measure, try to do it at the same time of year or term.

FURTHER SUGGESTIONS

Graph library attendance over time: by time of day, day of week, etc.

Compare library attendance to other regularly collected measures of use, such as Circulation. Our preliminary tests in a few sample libraries revealed no stable relationship in those libraries, but your library may be different. If library attendance is a constant proportion of, say, Circulation, you can estimate attendance from circulation counts.

Identify extremely "busy" times versus "slow" times and consider possible reasons for such variations.

8. Remote Uses

DEFINITION

Remote use is library use for which the user does not come to the library.

The kinds of remote uses vary across libraries. Each library should identify the kinds of remote uses relevant for it. Examples of remote use include:

- Document delivery services
- Access to library catalogs or other online databases maintained by the library from terminals outside the library
- Telephone, e-mail, or fax reference questions, requests for database searches, or other service requests.

A complete measure of library use should include remote use as well as attendance, because of the increasing use of technology to provide service to users at their locations instead of at the library.

DATA COLLECTION

1. Identify the kinds of remote uses relevant to your library.
2. Decide upon your data collection period. As with Attendance, Remote Use can be counted on an ongoing basis or during a sample period. See "Attendance, Data Collection," on page 77.
3. Count the number of remote uses of each kind. *Counting should be as consistent as possible and be parallel to the way the same kind of use is counted when the user comes to the library.* Some examples:

Document delivery services: each contact should be counted as a use. For example, if a user requests six titles simultaneously, that is one use; if the same user were to submit six separate requests at six different times, that is six uses. (If that user came to the library searching for six items on one visit, she or he would be counted once going through the turnstile. If the user came back six times, she or he would be counted six times.)

Dial-up access to online catalog: each catalog session counts as one use, regardless of the number of searches performed.

Reference/circulation services: all telephone, mail, e-mail, and fax service contacts should be counted. If an in-person user would have needed to come into the library (e.g., to renew a book, ask a directional question, etc.), then a remote user should be counted in the same way as the door counter would have counted the in-person user. Decide (for your situation) what is and is not a use. Consider whether a patron's asking for the library's hours on the phone is a use. What is important is that you are *consistent*.

DATA ANALYSIS

Libraries that count remote use on an ongoing basis may simply sum the data.

Libraries that sample remote use but keep continuous attendance records may consider projecting an annual total for remote use. Although we have no empirical evidence to support this, it seems reasonable that Remote Use would correlate with Attendance. If you wish to project to an annual total, divide Remote Use by Attendance during the sample period to calculate Remote Use as a percentage of Attendance. Then multiply this percentage by your total Attendance to derive the Annual Remote Use.

Example: During a sample period of 1 week a library has 425 remote uses and 3,615 in-library uses. Total attendance for the year is 165,712. The total Remote Uses would be projected as:

$$425/3615 = .118$$
$$.118 \times 165{,}712 = 19{,}885 \text{ Remote Uses}$$

Relating Remote Use to Attendance assumes that Remote Use is a constant proportion of Attendance, which may or may not be the case. You can test this assumption by counting Remote Use at various times and comparing it to Attendance.

DISCUSSION	Libraries are using technology to provide more convenient service, which increasingly means remote service. Users no longer have to come to the library to search the catalogs, request materials, ask reference questions, request database searches, etc. Not only do traditional use measures (such as Attendance) therefore underestimate use, a decrease in such traditional measures may actually represent an improvement in service, as use becomes more convenient via these technologies. It is necessary, therefore, for libraries to distinguish between decreases in traditional library use measures brought about by decreases in services versus those brought about by improved convenience.

Different remote uses are possible in different libraries. Not all remote uses are countable. Remote use of online catalogs, for example, can be counted only if the system has been programmed appropriately. And if much of this use is by the library staff, reporting it as patron use would be misleading.

Remote Use is particularly likely to be noncomparable across libraries, due to differences in the kinds of remote uses possible and the feasibility of counting them.

FURTHER SUGGESTIONS	Calculate Remote Use as a percentage of Attendance (see above).

Calculate Remote Use as a percentage of Circulation.

Analyze Remote Use over time: by time of day, day of week, week of the academic term, etc.

Analyze Remote Use by type of use or location.

9. Total Uses

DEFINITION	Total uses of the library, in-person and remote.

DATA ANALYSIS	Sum the tallies for Attendance and Remote Uses. This measure may be reported for a specific sample period of time or as an annual total, depending on the Attendance and Remote Use data available.

DISCUSSION | Total Uses reflect all use of the library, regardless of whether users came to the library. This approach is especially significant in libraries where Remote Use is large relative to Attendance.

This figure is rarely comparable across libraries, due to the difficulty of defining and measuring Remote Uses consistently. It may be important for tracking trends within a library over time, however, particularly where advances in technology and convenience of services mean that Remote Use is replacing Attendance.

FURTHER SUGGESTIONS | Analyze Total Use over time: by time of day, day of week, etc.

Compare Total Use to other regularly collected measures of use, such as Circulation.

Divide Total Use by the number of people in your primary user population to determine the number of uses per capita.

Analyze Total Use by types or location of uses.

10. Facilities Use Rate

DEFINITION | The proportion of time, on average, that a facility is busy. Another way to say this is that the Facilities Use Rate is the probability that a user will find a facility busy.

Facilities may include:

User seating, such as carrels, table seats, and lounge chairs

User workstations, such as computer terminals or microcomputers, including CD-ROM readers

Equipment such as photocopy machines and microfilm/fiche readers

Conference rooms, faculty study rooms, assigned study carrels

Compact shelving could be treated like equipment, since each user limits the access of others.

What all these facilities have in common is limited capacity. A user may find all facilities of the type needed unavailable.

BACKGROUND | A major library service is the provision of study space and equipment. In academic libraries, in particular, students rely on the library for a quiet space to study and for copy machines, computer terminals, and the like. Facilities provision is a useful service in itself as well as supporting people's use of other library resources.

In some academic libraries a large proportion of visitors is students studying their own materials. The most frequent subject of comments on the pretest user surveys for this manual, regardless of the focus of the survey, was facilities: lack of seats, noise, problems with copy machines, etc. For these students, the library's facilities are an important service in support of their academic program; for some, more important than the library's collection.

However, little previous work has addressed the measurement of facilities' availability and use. DeProspo and others (1973) present a method for measuring the utilization of equipment and facilities such as study space and copy machines. The replacement of card catalogs with online public access catalogs has required libraries to decide the number of terminals needed, resulting in queuing studies of catalog terminals (e.g., Tolle, Sanders, and Kaske, 1983).

Facilities Use Rate addresses the intensity of use of library facilities. The questions addressed are: What is the probability that a user will find a seat, a piece of equipment, or a public service staff member available? How heavily are existing facilities and equipment being used?

DATA COLLECTION

1. Determine which facilities are of interest for this measure.

   You need not collect utilization data for all facilities in the library; select only ones of interest.

   Only facilities *accessible to users* should be included. Those reserved exclusively for staff use are excluded.

   On Form 10-1, list the types of facilities in which you are interested and the number of each kind in the library. Consider how finely you wish the data broken down; for example, do you want a Facilities Use Rate for all photocopy machines together, or for each machine, department, floor, etc.? This determines how you group the facilities on Form 10-1. Smaller units are better than larger ones; you can always aggregate the data later but you cannot disaggregate it.

   All but the smallest libraries will need separate data collection forms for different spaces (e.g., one for each floor or department). The portion of the library covered by each form depends on how much space a person can cover when doing data collection, and how the data are to be reported (e.g., by floor, by subject department, by part of the collection, etc.).

   Facilities should be listed in the order in which the person doing the counting will encounter them.

2. Using Form 10-1, count the total number of each of the facilities available by category. (Form 10-1S is a worked example.)

   If the number varies (e.g., if you want to distinguish the number of copy machines operational at any time), instead of one column for "number available" on Form 10-1, count the number available each time you count the number in use.

3. At sampling times, a staff member walks quickly through the library counting on Form 10-1 the number of each type of facility in use.

   Count facilities, not users (e.g., two people sharing a terminal count as one). "In use" means unavailable to another user. For example, if an unoccupied study carrel contains a user's personal belongings so that a newcomer would not feel free to use it, it is in use.

   It helps if the same person collects data each time. The counting gets faster with practice; also, it will be consistent. An alarm (such as an alarm watch) is a useful reminder of when to count.

   A facility being used by a staff member is in use.

Form 10-1s
Facilities Data Collection Form

Department: _Reference_   Date: _10/31/89_   _1_ of _1_

Directions: At sampling time, go quickly through the library and count the number of people using each of the following.
Use Rate is Number in Use divided by Number Available.

OBSERVATIONS

Facilities	Number Available	Time: 9:15		Time: 10:15		Time: 11:15		Time: 12:15		Time: 1:15		Time: 2:15	
		# in Use	Use Rate*	# in Use	Use Rate	# in Use	Use Rate	# in Use	Use Rate	# in Use	Use Rate	# in Use	Use Rate
Table seats	8	4	.5	6	.75	8	1.0	6	.75	7	.88	4	.5
Online catalog terminals	2	1	.5	2	1.0	2	1.0	1	.5	2	1.0	2	1.0
Copy machines	2	2	1.0	2	1.0	2	1.0	1	.5	2	1.0	2	1.0
Index-table seats	4	1	.25	2	.5	3	.75	4	1.0	4	1.0	3	.75

*Divide # in Use by Number Available.

4. Divide the number of facilities in use by the number available to get the Facilities Use Rate for each type of facility for each time period.

Facilities Use Rates are derived from samples, and so are subject to sampling error (see Chapter 2). Reducing the sampling error requires a large number of observations, but in most libraries, Facilities Use varies considerably during the day, from day to day, and during the year or academic term. For example, in most academic libraries Facilities Use is low early in the term. Study space may be heavily used during exam periods. Use of online catalog terminals and CD-ROM indexes may be heaviest at peak term paper times.

Facilities Use, therefore, is a moving target. Instead of developing an overall Facilities Use Rate representative of an entire term, we recommend a "snapshot" approach. Pick a short period of time (a week or two) to collect data.

The choice of when to collect data depends on the information needed. For example, for an academic library:

- To determine Use Rates for a "typical" period, choose a period several weeks into the term, but not during midterms or finals, nor during the end-of-term paper rush (see Chapter 2).
- For Use Rates for peak periods, collect data during the busiest parts of the term and/or times of day.

Another approach is to collect data during several short periods to compare against one another (e.g., for a week each at the beginning, middle, and end of the term).

During the sample periods, collect data every hour, preferably at the same time past the hour (e.g., at 15 minutes past the hour). In deciding when during the hour to collect data, consider use patterns. For example, many academic libraries experience a flurry of visitors just before and after class times. Use figures collected during those times will be higher than at other times.

DATA ANALYSIS

To calculate Average Facilities Use Rate for each type of facility, total the individual Use Rates from all copies of Form 10-1 and divide by the number of Use Rates totaled. Report on Form 10-2 (Form 10-2S is an example).

Facilities Use Rates can be greater than or less than 1. For example, one person using a copy machine while two wait results in a Use Rate of 3.0 for that machine at that time. A machine that is busy half the time, with no one waiting, will have an Average Use Rate of 0.5.

For this measure, aggregating data may obscure important information. You may be more interested in how Facilities Use Rates change by time of day, day of week, etc.; if so, then average all the observations for that period of time.

Example: A library has two copy machines. Copy machine use rates during a single day were as follows:

9:15 am	.5
10:15 am	.5
11:15 am	1.0
12:15 pm	1.5 (one person waiting)

Form 10-2s
Average Facilities Rate Summary

Average Facilities Use Rate = Average of All Observations

Facilities	Number Available	Average Facilities Use Rate
Table seats	8	.73
Online catalog terminals	2	.83
Copy machines	2	.92
Index table seats	4	.71

1:15 pm	2.0 (two people waiting)
2:15 pm	.5
3:15 pm	.5
4:15 pm	1.0

The average Copy Machine Use Rate during this day was 0.94:

$$\frac{.5 + .5 + 1 + 1.5 + 2 + .5 + .5 + 1}{8} = .94$$

Alternatively, during a week of data collection the Copy Machine Use Rates at 12:15 pm (a time of heavy use) were:

Mon	1.5
Tues	2.0
Wed	1.5
Thurs	1.5
Fri	1.0

The average 12:15 pm Copy Machine Use Rate was:

$$\frac{1.5 + 2.0 + 1.5 + 1.5 + 1.0}{5} = 1.5$$

Averaging Use Rates for a given type of facility over hours of the day and/or days of the week will reveal busy times. For example:

- Average Use Rates over all Monday observations, compared to all Tuesday observations, reveal how busy Monday is relative to Tuesday.
- Comparing the average of all 9 am observations during the week to all 3 pm observations allows you to compare average 9 am use levels to 3 pm, and so forth.
- Graphing Use Rates over hours of the day and/or days of the week will reveal trends.

Similar facilities can be combined; for example, study carrels and table seating can be combined into study space. Do not average the Use Rates across the different types of facilities; instead, count the number available and the number used and calculate a new Use Rate for each time period.

DISCUSSION

The basic questions addressed by this measure are: What are the chances that a user will find a facility busy? How heavily are library facilities used?

Average Facilities Use Rate may be less useful than the rate during peak times. Can your library accommodate highest levels of demand?

In interpreting results, keep in mind that these are *estimates, with some margin of error.* Also consider the period during which the data were collected because results represent use only during that period.

Note also that Facilities Use Rates may not reflect total demand. For example, people may not wait for a copy machine but do other things while watching for the machine to be free. Other users may become discouraged and leave without using the machine.

Each library has to decide what is an appropriate Use Rate for each kind of facility. It may be more acceptable, for example, to have people queued for copy machines than for online catalog terminals or users may wait for copy machines and terminals, but what will they do when they find all the chairs full?

A high Facilities Use Rate means that that facility is busy. A low Use Rate means it is not very busy. High rates may indicate a need to expand capacity. Low rates may indicate excess capacity. Some ways of improving service include:

- Designate "express" online catalog terminals for searches of two minutes or less.
- Add temporary seating during high-use periods, such as final exams.
- Rearrange space to discourage individuals from taking excess space by putting their feet on chairs, etc.
- Replace underutilized facilities with added capacity for those that are

heavily utilized. For example, move study carrels from less to more busy areas.

- Use these data to support budget requests for equipment, as needed.

FURTHER SUGGESTIONS	Analyze data by day of week and/or by time of day.

Analyze data throughout the library by type of facility (e.g., type of seating). This may reveal patterns of use, for example, preferred types of seating, useful for space planning.

Calculate the proportion of time that a facility is busy, ignoring the number of people waiting. For example, if there are two copy machines, count the proportion of observations equal to or greater than two—that is, the proportion of time that a third user would find both machines already occupied.

Compare number or proportion of seats filled for different types of seating to see which kind of seating is most used.

11. Service Point Use

DEFINITION	The average number of users at a service point.

Service points are staffed public service sites (e.g., circulation, reference, and information desks). Service points differ from facilities in that:

- They are staffed.
- They do not necessarily have a fixed capacity (staffing levels may not be fixed). For example, staff may help at the desk when it is busy, then go back to nondesk duties. And staff may sometimes serve more than one user at a time.

Where service points *do* have fixed capacity (e.g., a circulation desk with fixed staffing), Service Point Use can be calculated in exactly the same way as Facilities Use Rate, on Form 10-1.

BACKGROUND	Another area besides physical facilities in which availability and queues are issues is service desks. Staff assistance is an important library service, not only reference service but circulation control, materials paging, and the like. Queues reduce library costs by imposing an added time cost on the user, essentially shifting costs from the library to the user (Van House, 1983) by making library use slower and less convenient.

DATA COLLECTION	The method followed is identical to that for Facilities Use. At selected sample times staff walk through the library and count the number of users at each service point. Use Form 11-1.

Form 11-1s
Service Point Data Collection Form

Department: _Main_

Date: _10/31/89_

Directions: At sampling time, go quickly through the library and count the number of users at each of the following service points. Count both users being served and those waiting.

Service Points	Time:	Time:	Time:	Time:	Time:	Time:	Time:	Time:	Time:	Time: N/A	Average
Reference Desk	1	2	3	3	4	4	3	2	0		2.44
Info Desk	0	1	2	2	3	6	2	0	1		1.88
Circ Desk	2	4	0	3	2	0	5	2	1		2.11
Total											

DATA ANALYSIS

The hourly numbers of people at each service point are probably of the most interest, and these can be graphed over time (see Figure 2-6). You may also calculate the average number of users at each service point, including people being served as well as those waiting for service. Use Form 11-2.

Unlike Facilities Use Rate, you cannot measure the proportion of the staff available who are busy, because of the fluidity of staffing and the possibility that staff serve more than one person at a time.

DISCUSSION

In staffing service points, most libraries seek a balance so that staff are readily available but are rarely unoccupied for any length of time. Library users tend to arrive irregularly, varying the load on each service point.

Users are often reluctant to wait, so Service Point Use may understate the

Form 11-2S
Service Point Summary

Service Points	Average Number of Users
Reference Desk	2.44
Info Desk	1.88
Circ Desk	2.11

demand on a service point. For example, some people will not wait at the reference desk, but will do other things while waiting for a librarian. Other users will be discouraged and not seek assistance.

FURTHER SUGGESTIONS

Analyze data by day of week and/or by time of day; this can be used to match staffing to demand.

Calculate the proportion of time that a service point is busy, ignoring the number of people waiting. Calculate the proportion of observations that is equal to or greater than the number of staff normally assigned. This is the probability that a user would find a staff member available.

Calculate the proportion of observations for which there are one, two, three, etc., users at a service point. Compare this to staffing levels at the same service point.

12. Building Use

DEFINITION

Average number of people in the library at any one time.

For a different approach to measuring number of library users, see measure 7, "Attendance," above. These measures are different, but similar enough that you may not wish to do both.

DATA COLLECTION

At selected sample times, staff walk through the library and count all the users in the library, using Form 12-1. The method followed is the same as that for Facilities Use Rate and Service Point Use (above), except that this time you are counting *all* users. Be sure to count people in the stacks and other hard-to-find spots. This is most feasible for small libraries (including branch libraries), but could be used in large libraries as well, by dividing the library into spaces of manageable size for counting.

This is best done by someone who knows the staff, so that they are sure to be counting only users, not staff members.

The choice of sample times is discussed under "Facilities Use Rate," above.

DATA ANALYSIS

Total the number of people in the library at each count. You can then average these totals over your observations to get the average number of people using the library, although the hour-by-hour totals may be more informative. These can be graphed, as in Figure 2-6. You may also want to average your findings by time of day and/or part of the library—that is, average all the counts taken at 9 am (etc.) or average all the counts of users in a particular area. Use Form 12-2.

Building Use can be combined with Facilities Use Rate and Service Point Use by counting all users, but differentiating whether each person counted is

Form 12-1s
Building Use Data Collection Form

Library: _Branch_   Date: _10/31_   _1_ of _2_

Number of Users

Space	Time:	Time:	Time:	Time:	Time:	Time:	Time:	Time:	Time:	Time:	Time:	Time:
Reference Area	2	3	3	3	4	3	3	2	4	4	1	0
Stacks	3	4	7	8	9	6	4	5	3	2	1	1
Reading Room	1	1	2	5	7	8	9	4	5	4	4	4
Total	6	8	12	16	20	17	16	11	12	10	6	5

Average number of users: _____
(average totals)

Form 12-2 s
Building Use Summary

Space	Average Number of Users
Reference Area	3.2
Stacks	5.1
Reading Room	6.0

(1) using a facility such as a workstation or study space, (2) at a service point, or (3) "other," such as browsing in the stacks.

DISCUSSION

This measure indicates the average use of library facilities by reporting the number of people in the library at any given time. Attendance gives the total number passing through the library over a period of time; and this measure gives the average number in the library at a point in time.

FURTHER SUGGESTIONS

Calculate your average Building Use as a percent of the people in your primary user population. You may be able to say that, at any given time, an average X% of the population of your campus (institution, department, etc.) are in the library.

Divide Average Building Use by the number of public service staff on the desks at any given time to get the ratio of users to staff.

Calculate the ratio of Average Building Use to user seats—workstations, study space, etc.

INFORMATION SERVICES

With the rapid change in the nature of bibliographic sources, library patrons are increasingly dependent on information specialists to help them determine the most efficient and effective methods of locating the information they need. Information or reference services serve as a gateway for library users. The quality of reference service sets the tone of many academic libraries.

It is difficult to measure the levels of effort expended and the success of information services. Numerous measures of reference service success have been proposed. Powell (1984) presents an excellent review of the reference-effectiveness literature. The proposed measures of reference service can be divided into four broad categories:

- Enumerations of the quantity of reference service (e.g., Center for Education Statistics, 1988)
- Objective measures of the accuracy of information provided, usually based on the assessment of an objective judge (Lancaster, 1988; Hernon and McClure, 1987; Van House and Childers, 1984)

- Librarians' evaluation of reference outcome (Kantor, 1981; Van House and others, 1987; Whitlatch, 1987, 1989)
- User's subjective evaluation of reference outcome (Murfin and Gugelchuk, 1987; Whitlatch, 1987).

This manual attempts to reach a balance between the quantitative and subjective aspects of information services. Reference Transactions measures the number of reference transactions. The Reference Satisfaction Survey focuses on the users' satisfaction with the outcome and nature of the service provided.

The outcome of the reference transaction has three components: relevance of the information provided, satisfaction with the amount of information provided, and the completeness of the answer received. The nature of the reference transaction is important because the reference transaction may have been successful, but the user may be dissatisfied with either the difficulty of reaching a successful outcome or the service experience.

13. Reference Transactions

DEFINITION

The total number of reference transactions during a period of time. A reference transaction is an information contact that involves the knowledge, use, recommendations, interpretation, or instruction in the use of one or more information sources by a member of the library staff. Information sources include printed and nonprinted materials, machine-readable databases (including computer-assisted instruction, catalogs and other holdings records), thorough communication or referral, other libraries and institutions, and persons both inside and outside the library.

If a contact includes both reference and directional services, it should be reported as one reference transaction. Duration should not be an element in determining whether a transaction is a reference transaction.

This definition is the same as that for the Integrated Postsecondary Education Data System (IPEDS). Use your IPEDS data, if available.

Note that many transactions which facilitate the use of the library do not involve the knowledge, use, recommendation, interpretation, or instruction in the use of any information sources. Do not count these as reference transactions. Some examples of interactions which should *not* be included are giving directions for locating staff, users, physical features within the library, or providing assistance (of a nonbibliographic nature) with machines.

BACKGROUND

Libraries have adopted a variety of methods of collecting information service statistics. Generally this involves counting and often categorizing the reference questions received in person or by phone or mail. Kesselman and Watstein (1987) note the growing literature concerning reference statistics and its increasing importance in the management of academic and research libraries. Sampling methodologies are provided by Kesselman and Watstein (1987) and by Halperin (1974). Because these methodologies require measurement over a minimum of thirty days and a level of knowledge of statistics not routinely utilized by librarians, this manual has not used their methodologies.

The Reference Transactions measure provides data that tell how many reference questions were handled. It does not answer the questions "how well" or "how accurately." Quality of reference service may be measured by "correct answer fill rate" which is discussed in great detail in Hernon and McClure (1987). The Reference Satisfaction Survey surveys the users' perception of satisfaction.

DATA COLLECTION

Staff collect data by using Form 13-1, or by a form of your own design. (See Form 13-1 [Form 13-1S is an example] and the discussion on sampling in Chapter 2.)

Reference service takes place at a variety of service desks; so consider the appropriate service desks to evaluate. Depending on the number of reference

Form 13-1
Reference Services Statistics
Daily Desk Reporting Form

Name: _Biology Library_   Date: _12/3/89_
May be a department, unit, or individual (as appropriate)

Hour	Reference	Total
8 – 9	I	1
9 – 11	HHT I	6
11 – 1	HHT HHT II	12
1 – 3	HHT HHT HHT HHT HHT II	27
3 – 5	HHT HHT HHT III	18
5 – 7	HHT HHT	10
7 – 9		
9 –		

Total: _74_

transactions at each desk, information, circulation, and media center desks may be appropriate. It may be more difficult to count at desks with a relatively low proportion of reference transactions. Not including these service points may leave out important performance data. Documenting your decisions makes data comparisons feasible in future years.

Consider recording questions answered by staff when they are not officially "on the desk." In small branch libraries without reference desks, these questions must be counted. In larger libraries, staff sometimes wish to include questions asked in corridors on the way to lunch.

Ensure that all participating staff are aware of the definition of a reference question. Distribute examples of what is and is not considered a reference question at a staff meeting and discuss them. Ask staff for other possibilities and add them to the list. If reference services are provided through several departments, include representatives from as many departments as possible.

Two approaches to counting questions are possible:

1. *Annual count.* Many libraries already count the number of reference transactions handled each year for reporting to various agencies or for internal use. Use these data if available. Although some organizations may define reference transactions differently from the IPEDS definition recommended here, do not change the definition you are using. Consistency in the library is necessary— and more important than consistency with our definition.

Staff tend to forget to mark down reference questions and estimate them at the end of the shift, day, week, or month. The best accuracy is obtained when staff tally questions as they receive them. As shifts change, incoming staff should ensure that those leaving the desk have recorded their questions.

2. *Sampling.* If a library does not currently count reference transactions on an ongoing basis, the data can be collected by sampling. Sampling may be more accurate than an ongoing count.

Select a sample period. The period during which you collect data will determine your results. The simplest solution is to pick a reasonably representative time period—that is, a busy time but (in academic libraries) not during midterms or finals or periods of other unusual activity (see Chapter 2).

During the sample period ask library staff to count reference transactions at all relevant service points.

We recommend that you collect data all the hours that reference service is provided, for one or preferably two weeks.

DATA ANALYSIS

In a library where all reference transactions handled throughout the year are counted, simply total the number of reference questions.

In a library that counts reference questions during a sample period, it is difficult to project one or two weeks' data to an entire academic year. Analysis of data from academic libraries which count their reference questions continuously indicates that extrapolating from a one- or two-week sample to an annual total does not consistently give accurate results. We recommend, instead, that the data be reported for the period of time it is collected. That is, report that, during the week(s) of _____, reference assistance was provided X number of times.

DISCUSSION	The number of reference transactions is an indicator of the level of use of a library. High numbers of reference transactions, combined with high overall user satisfaction, may be indicative of good reference service. High numbers of reference transactions, combined with overall low levels of user satisfaction, may indicate that the reference service is very busy, but patrons' needs are not being met. Examining the kinds of reference questions asked most frequently may suggest ideas for helping users to become more self-sufficient.

A low number of reference questions, combined with low user overall satisfaction, may indicate the need for a more active reference service. Some possibilities for increasing the number of reference transactions include relocating the desk to a more prominent place in the library, advertising reference services offered, encouraging the staff to be more active in offering assistance, examining bibliographic instruction programs, and increasing services offered. Changing staffing levels, the times that service is offered, or policies and procedures may also help.

To determine the average rate of reference use, see the Service Point Utilization measure.

FURTHER SUGGESTIONS

Analyze data by service points to find the most heavily used service points.

Divide the total number of Reference Transactions during the year or sample period by the number of:

Total Uses during the year or sample period, to determine the ratio of reference questions received to library uses

FTE staff available to provide service, to measure the workload per staff member

hours that reference service is available during the period, to determine how extensively the service is used

staff hours of reference service to measure the average workload per hour per individual at the reference desk.

Compare the annual number of reference transactions to cost data for the provision of reference service.

Analyze your own historical data. Compare a proposed sample week's data and consider: "Had we used those figures and multiplied by the appropriate number of weeks to project to the semester or annual total, how close would the result have been to the actual total?" It is necessary to compare several years of data. Our preliminary tests in a few sample libraries varied drastically. If the number of reference transactions is relatively stable, the data may prove that a particular two-week period may be used to estimate the total.

Record data by day of week and time of day or week of academic term to find periods of high use.

Categorize questions by type as staff record them. Examples might be catalog assistance, term paper, end-user searching.

14. Reference Satisfaction Survey

DEFINITION

Users' self-reports of:

a) Outcome of the reference transaction (i.e., users' report of how well the question was answered)
b) Service experience (e.g., was staff member helpful, quality of the service provided)
c) Overall satisfaction with the reference service.

Questions 1 to 3 on Form 14-1 address the users' satisfaction with the outcome of the reference transaction by evaluating the relevance and satisfaction with the amount of information provided and the completeness of the answer received.

Question 4 addresses the manner of the interaction. The reference transaction could have been successful, but user may be dissatisfied with the difficulty of reaching a successful outcome. This question evaluates the helpfulness of the staff assistance.

Question 5 asks patrons to provide their overall assessment of the reference service. Since the importance of the outcome and nature of the reference transaction will vary among patrons, it is important to measure the component parts and to ask for an overall assessment.

BACKGROUND

Although there is a considerable amount of literature concerning reference effectiveness, few academic libraries have attempted to quantify the success of their reference efforts.

The effectiveness of reference service is affected by a number of factors (Hernon and McClure, 1987), including:

- Size and type of collection
- Staff social and technical skills and competencies
- Physical organization and location of materials
- Bibliographic control over materials
- Technical support (i.e., online services, microcomputers, etc.)
- Organizational climate and management style
- Information needs of clientele
- Financial support
- Physical accessibility of the reference service (e.g., building location, reference hours, number of available staff).

Murfin and Gugelchuk (1987) have developed a two-page questionnaire which takes into account multiple dimensions of the reference transaction. The goals of their questionnaire include:

- Control possible bias in favor of librarian by effectively separating ratings of service from those of success in finding what was wanted
- Prevent blurring of the rating of success with other outcomes by providing separate ratings for:

Form 14-1
Reference Satisfaction Survey

PLEASE LET US KNOW HOW WE ARE DOING. Evaluate the *reference* service that you received today by circling one number on each of the following scales. Feel free to explain—use the back of the form.

If you were NOT asking a reference question today, please check here ____ and stop. Thank you.

1. *Relevance* of information provided:

   Not relevant   1   2   3   4   5   Very relevant

2. Satisfaction with the *amount* of information provided:

   Not satisfied   1   2   3   4   5   Very satisfied
   (too little, too much)   (the right amount)

3. *Completeness* of the answer that you received:

   Not complete   1   2   3   4   5   Very complete

4. *Helpfulness* of staff:

   Not helpful   1   2   3   4   5   Extraordinarily helpful

5. Overall, how *satisfied* are you?

   Not satisfied   1   2   3   4   5   Extremely satisfied

Why? _____

_____

6. You are:

   ____ 1. Undergraduate   ____ 4. Research staff
   ____ 2. Graduate student   ____ 5. Other staff
   ____ 3. Faculty   ____ 6. Other?_____

7. What will you use this information for?

   ____ 1. Course work   ____ 4. Mix of several purposes
   ____ 2. Research   ____ 5. Current awareness
   ____ 3. Teaching   ____ 6. Other?_____

THANK YOU! Please leave this questionnaire in the box.

USE BACK OF PAGE FOR ANY ADDITIONAL COMMENTS.

Success in finding what was wanted
Satisfaction with the information/materials found or not found
Satisfaction with service (helpfulness, etc.), amount learned, and communication difficulty

Whitlatch (1987) proposed measures for

- Relevance of information provided
- Amount of information provided
- Quality of service provided
- Overall satisfaction.

The Reference Satisfaction Survey asks users to evaluate

- Relevance of information provided
- Amount of information provided
- Completeness of the answer received
- Helpfulness of staff
- Overall satisfaction

This measure will provide data for managers indicating the patron's level of satisfaction with these aspects of the information service. The measure is not intended to diagnose the causes of failure. For this, readers are referred to Murfin and Gugelchuk (1987), Hernon and McClure (1987), and Kantor (1981).

DATA COLLECTION

For the Reference Satisfaction Survey, use Form 14-1; see instructions for User Survey (Chapter 3) and the discussion on sampling and sample sizes (Chapter 2).

Reference service takes place at a variety of service desks. Consider the appropriate service desks to evaluate. Depending on the number of reference transactions at each desk, information, circulation, and media center desks may be included. It may be more difficult to administer the questionnaire at desks with a low proportion of reference transactions. Not including these service points may, however, skew data or leave out important performance data. (For a definition of a reference transaction, see the Reference Transactions Measure.)

The evaluation of reference service frequently appears to staff and patrons to be a personnel evaluation. Before doing this measure, it is recommended that the reference staff meet and the importance, need, and process for obtaining the data are explained. It is important for the staff to know that the service is being evaluated, not individuals, and specifically why the evaluation is being done. The best results are obtained when staff participate in the evaluation process and when staff know why the evaluation is being done.

Form 14-1, question 7, lists the major uses that we have identified for some sample academic libraries. Consider whether this list is appropriate for your library. The demographic categories (question 6) may also need revision for your library.

Generally, you will want to survey at least 100 users who engaged in reference transactions during their visit to the library. Considerably more, up to 400, is preferable. Users are quite cooperative; a response rate of 85 percent is common. However, most libraries find it more difficult to get large numbers of responses to the reference survey than to other surveys because reference service users are a small proportion of total library users.

Plan to distribute the survey for one to three weeks. Reference transaction data can be utilized to estimate how long you will need to distribute surveys. For example, if the library typically receives 50 reference transactions each day, with a response rate of 85 percent, 42 surveys per day may be returned. To receive 400 surveys, data should be collected for 10 days. Collecting data for longer than three weeks is generally not recommended. Repeat users will resist filling out the survey forms and your response rate will drop.

During the sample period each user is asked to help improve library service by filling out a short questionnaire. Some of the same patrons will be asked on more than one occasion to complete a questionnaire. This is important since they are evaluating the reference service that they received *at that time*. Their perception of the service may well be different on various occasions. We are sampling reference transactions, not patrons.

Have staff—other than the service staff—distribute the questionnaire. Station a staff member in front of the desk, near enough to hear the question but far enough away to not interfere with service. Staff should try not to give questionnaires to people asking directional questions. (If questionnaires are given to patrons asking directional questions, you may need more forms to reach your target number of questionnaires.) The staff distributing the questions need to be persuasive. In particular, they should persuade patrons to fill out the survey before leaving the library or (in large libraries) the reference area.

DATA ANALYSIS

Summarize the number of times each possible answer was given to each question on the questionnaire. Use Form 14-3 as a guide (Form 14-3S is a completed example). User surveys may be tabulated manually or by computer (see Chapter 2).

Before tabulating, the questionnaires should be reviewed as described in Chapter 3, "User Surveys," for possible tabulation problems. If a questionnaire is hopelessly confused and cannot be tabulated, simply count it as "not usable." If an answer is unclear, or the respondent circles more than one answer to a question, do not infer what you think the user meant. If an answer cannot be tabulated as the user reported it, it is "missing."

A questionnaire that indicates that the user did not use the reference service should be treated as "not usable" because it does not represent an evaluation of the reference service.

The answers to the open-ended "why" questions make for interesting reading. If you wish to tabulate them, read through enough questionnaires to define some recurring reasons, then count the number of times each type of reason is given.

Form 14-2 (Reference Satisfaction Survey Tabulation) can be used to tabulate the Reference Satisfaction Survey manually. Any changes to Form 14-1 will require corresponding changes in Forms 14-2 through 14-4.

Record each questionnaire on a separate line on Form 14-2. The number of lines filled is the number of questionnaires tabulated.

You can also simply count for each question the number of times each answer is reported, without tabulating each questionnaire on a separate line as Form 14-2 does. The advantage to Form 14-2 is that you can go back and select subsets of questionnaires; for example, you can find all the responses from faculty and analyze those separately.

If the answers to some questions (but not all) are unclear or missing, draw a line through the space for tabulating that answer. You'll want to be able to come back and count the number of questions with missing answers. If an entire questionnaire is unusable, count in the "not usable" box on Form 14-2.

Library_____

No.___ of___
Sample Period_____

Form 14-2
Reference Satisfaction Survey Tabulation

#	Relevance					Amount					Completeness					Helpfulness					Overall					Status							Purpose						
	1	2	3	4	5	1	2	3	4	5	1	2	3	4	5	1	2	3	4	5	1	2	3	4	5	U	G	F	R	S	O	C	R	T	CA	M	O
Page Total																																					

Not usable:

Form 14-3s
Reference Satisfaction Survey Worksheet

1. Relevance (Compute totals from bottom of Form 14-2)

(1)	(2) Number	(3) Percent[1]	(4) (1) × (2)
1	0	0	0
2	0	0	0
3	4	4	12
4	19	20	76
5	73	76	365
Total	96	100%	453
No answer[2]	5		

Average (divide Total from column 4 by Total from column 2): __4.7__

[1]Enter these percentages on Form 14-4.
[2]Do not use this number in calculating percentages.

2. Amount (Compute totals from bottom of Form 14-2)

(1)	(2) Number	(3) Percent[1]	(4) (1) × (2)
1	1	1	1
2	4	4	8
3	7	7	21
4	21	22	84
5	64	66	320
Total	97	100%	434
No answer[2]	4		

Average (divide Total from column 4 by Total from column 2): __4.4__

[1]Enter these percentages on Form 14-4.
[2]Do not use this number in calculating percentages.

3. Completeness (Compute totals from bottom of Form 14-2)

(1)	(2) Number	(3) Percent[1]	(4) (1) × (2)
1	0	0	0
2	2	2	4
3	8	8	24
4	25	26	100
5	62	64	310
Total	97	100%	438
No answer[2]	4		

Average (divide Total from column 4 by Total from column 2): __4.5__

[1]Enter these percentages on Form 14-4.
[2]Do not use this number in calculating percentages.

4. Helpfulness (Compute totals from bottom of Form 14-2)

(1)	(2) Number	(3) Percent[1]	(4) (1) × (2)
1	0	0	0
2	0	0	0
3	4	4	12
4	26	27	104
5	67	69	335
Total	97	100%	451
No answer[2]	4		

Average (divide Total from column 4 by Total from column 2): __4.6__

[1]Enter these percentages on Form 14-4.
[2]Do not use this number in calculating percentages.

Form 14-3 s
Reference Satisfaction Survey Worksheet (pg. 2)

5. Overall (Compute totals from bottom of Form 14-2)

(1)	(2) Number	(3) Percent[1]	(4) (1) × (2)
1	1	1	1
2	2	2	4
3	4	4	12
4	27	28	108
5	62	64	310
Total	96	100%	435
No answer[2]	5		

Average(divideTotal from column 4
by Total from column 2): 4-5

[1]Enter these percentages on Form 14-4.
[2]Do not use this number in calculating
 percentages.

6. Status of Respondents (Compute totals from bottom
 of Form 14-2)

Status	Number	Percent[1]
1. Undergraduates	32	33
2. Graduate students	38	40
3. Faculty	4	4
4. Research staff	2	2
5. Other staff	3	3
6. Other	17	18
Total	96	100%
No answer[2]	5	

[1]Enter these percentages on Form 14-4.
[2]Do not use this number in calculating percentages.

7. Purpose (Compute totals from bottom of Form 14-2)

Purpose	Number	Percent[1]
1. Course work	27	28
2. Research	34	36
3. Teaching	2	2
4. Current awareness	5	5
5. Mix of purpose	10	11
6. Other	16	17
Total	94	100%
No answer[2]	7	

[1]Enter these percentages on Form 14-4.
[2]Do not use this number in calculating percentages.

Compute totals at the bottom of each copy of the tabulation form, then add the totals from the copies of the form and record on Form 14-3, the Reference Satisfaction Survey Worksheet.

Code a few questionnaires on Form 14-2 and then tabulate them on Form 14-3 before you do all the questionnaires—just to be sure that you understand what you are doing.

Whether you tabulate the surveys manually or by computer you will do the same basic analyses. The computer will allow you to do additional analyses with ease. Forms 14-3 and 14-4 will guide manual analysis (Forms 14-3S and 14-4S are worked examples). When using a computer, use Form 14-4 as a guide for the analyses that you need.

Form 14-4s
Summary of Results of Reference Satisfaction Survey

1. Number of questionnaires distributed:_____
2. Number of questionnaires returned and usable:_____
3. Response rate:_____
   (Divide line 2 by line 1)
4. Number of respondents not asking for reference assistance:_____
5. Number of questionnaires reporting on reference satisfaction:_____

Measure \ Rank	1	2	3	4	5	Average
Relevance						
Amount						
Completeness						
Helpfulness						
Overall						

Status of Respondents

Undergraduates	Graduate students	Faculty	Research staff	Other staff	Other	Total
						100%

# of responses _____ (Total, Table 6, Form 14-3)

Purpose

Course work	Research	Teaching	Current awareness	Mix of purposes	Other	Total
						100%

# of responses _____ (Total, Table 7, Form 14-3)

1. For each question, count the *frequency* with which each value appears, that is, the number of 1's, 2's, etc., circled for each. Also count the number of times the question was left blank.
2. Calculate the *percentage* of 1's, 2's, etc., for each item. Exclude from percentages the people who didn't answer the question.
3. Calculate the *average* score for the library. Again, exclude "missing" answers. (Note that for questions 6 and 7 an average would make no sense.)

DISCUSSION

Users' assessment of the success of their reference transaction depends on many factors, including the outcome of the transaction, their expectations of the reference service, the library's resources, the staff's behavior, the busyness of the library, the user's own efforts, availability of the information they were looking for, and the importance to the user of the information requested.

Reference satisfaction will never be 100 percent, and some reference answers do not exist. Some patrons will not be satisfied with the correct answers to their questions. Some users will report success when the librarian might not, and vice versa. Some users will be unrealistically critical of the service; some will be overly forgiving. Although these situations arise, they are generally a small percentage of the returned reference evaluation questionnaires.

Reference staff will be concerned about these issues. Discussing the expectations with them ahead of time may help them feel less threatened.

The majority of patrons rate their satisfaction with reference service very highly. Obviously, reference staff know they are being evaluated and are giving their best. However, it is not uncommon for patrons to mark that they are extremely satisfied with the reference service, even when they have indicated that their reference question was not answered. Frequently the most interesting and useful information comes from "odd ball" questionnaires and the written comments.

Users' self-reports of reference success provide valuable information about how the users view their reference transactions.

FURTHER SUGGESTIONS

Analyze data by service point by labeling or color coding questionnaires, and measure patron satisfaction in different service areas.

Cross-tabulate the answers to questions 1 to 5 with status, purpose, and/or use.

Use the questionnaire as the basis for an exit interview. Elicit more information from patrons concerning why or why not the service they received was satisfactory.

Analyze respondents who scored reference satisfaction as 1 or 2 ("unsatisfactory") and those "very satisfied" (4 or 5) as separate groups to see the differences between "more" and "less satisfied" respondents.

15. Online Search Evaluation

DEFINITION	Users' self-reports of:

a) Satisfaction with the performance of the search intermediary
b) Satisfaction with the search product
c) Overall satisfaction with the online search.

Questions 1 and 2 on Form 15-1 address the users' satisfaction with the performance of the search intermediary by evaluating the searcher's understanding of the search request and the thoroughness of the searcher in selecting databases and using relevant terms.

Questions 3 through 5 address the users' satisfaction with the product of the search, including the relevance, amount, and currency of the information provided.

Question 6 addresses the users' satisfaction with the length of time taken to provide the product. This is one part of evaluating the service experience of the user.

Question 7 asks patrons to provide their overall assessment of the online search. The importance of the variables will vary among patrons; therefore, it is important to measure the component parts and to ask for an overall assessment.

BACKGROUND	Initially, online searching evaluators placed the greatest emphasis on the objective measures of the search product, such as system performance and the precision and recall of the search (Lancaster, 1977). Increasingly greater emphasis has been placed on subjective measures concerning:

- Searcher performance (Auster, 1983; Auster and Lawton, 1984; Tessier and others, 1977)
- The search product (Tagliacozzo, 1977; Blood, 1983; Hilchey and Hurych, 1985).

Hilchey and Hurych (1985) broadened the perspective, previously narrowly defined as "the search," to the library as a whole, suggesting that there are four factors affecting user satisfaction with online searching:

- Output
- Interaction with the intermediary
- Service policies
- Library as a whole.

Lancaster (1988) suggests asking the patron to provide both subjective and objective evaluation of the search by asking patrons to judge the value of the search and provide data on the number of pertinent citations. Although this provides useful data, obtaining the high level of patron participation necessary for such a detailed analysis is difficult.

This approach focuses on the users' subjective evaluation of the:

- Searcher's performance
- Search product
- Service experience
- Overall satisfaction.

DATA COLLECTION

The user survey, Form 15-1, Online Search Evaluation, is distributed with completed searches at the time the search is received by the patron. Ask patrons to complete the questionnaires and place them in a box after the patrons have reviewed their search results. Simply distributing the forms and asking respondents to mail them back may drop response rate to 50 percent or less. Phone follow-up may be used to encourage the return of ques-

Form 15-1
Online Search Evaluation

PLEASE LET US KNOW HOW WE ARE DOING. Please indicate your satisfaction with the following aspects of your *online search* by CIRCLING a number on each of the following scales.

How satisfied are you with:

1. Searcher's *understanding* of your search request (main concept identified in developing the search strategy)?

    Not satisfied   1   2   3   4   5   Very satisfied

2. *Thoroughness* of the searcher in selecting appropriate database(s) and using relevant terms of phrases to retrieve references?

    Not satisfied   1   2   3   4   5   Very satisfied

3. *Relevance* of information provided?

    Not satisfied   1   2   3   4   5   Very satisfied

4. *Amount* of information provided (from your knowledge of the amount available in published sources)?

    Not satisfied   1   2   3   4   5   Very satisfied
    (too little, too much)   (the right amount)

    If not satisfied, please check: ____Too little ____Too much

5. *Currency* (up-to-dateness) of the information?

    Not satisfied   1   2   3   4   5   Very satisfied

6. *Time* taken to provide bibliography?

    Not satisfied   1   2   3   4   5   Very satisfied

7. Overall, how *satisfied* are you with the online search?

    Not satisfied   1   2   3   4   5   Very satisfied
    Why? _____

8. You are:

    ____1. Undergraduate   ____3. Faculty   ____5. Other staff
    ____2. Graduate student   ____4. Research staff   ____6. Other ?_____

9. What will you use this information for?

    ____1. Course work   ____3. Teaching   ____5. Several purposes
    ____2. Research   ____4. Current awareness   ____6. Other ?_____

Feel free to explain; please use the back of the page.

tionnaires, if you include patron names on them and record who has returned them. However, the loss of confidentiality may inhibit negative responses.

Form 15-1, question 9, lists the major uses that we have identified for some sample academic libraries. Consider whether this list is appropriate for your library. The demographic categories (question 8) may also need revision for your library.

Generally, you will want to survey at least 100 users who requested online searches. However, most libraries find it difficult to get this number of responses to the Online Search Evaluation because the number of online searches performed is small. To obtain a snapshot of how users evaluate your service, consider evaluating all searches for one month.

DATA ANALYSIS

Summarize the number of times each possible answer was given to each question on the questionnaire. (Use Form 15-3 as a guide.) User surveys may be tabulated manually or by computer (see Chapter 2).

Before tabulating, the questionnaires should be reviewed as described in Chapter 3, "User Surveys," for possible tabulation problems. If a questionnaire is hopelessly confused and cannot be tabulated, simply count it as "not usable." If an answer is unclear or the respondent circles more than one answer to a question, do not infer what you think the user meant. If an answer cannot be tabulated as the user reported it, it is "missing."

The answers to question 4's "too much/too little" and the open-ended "why" questions make for interesting reading. If you wish to tabulate them, read through enough questionnaires to define some recurring reasons, then count the number of times each type of reason is given.

Form 15-2 (Online Search Evaluation Tabulation) can be used to tabulate the Online Search Evaluation Form manually. Record each questionnaire on a separate line on Form 15-2. The number of lines filled is the number of questionnaires tabulated.

You can also simply count (for each question) the number of times each answer is reported, without tabulating each questionnaire on a separate line as Form 15-2 does. The advantage to Form 15-2 is that you can go back and select subsets of questionnaires. For example, you can find all the responses from graduate students and analyze those separately.

If the answers to some questions (but not all) are unclear or missing, draw a line through the spaces for tabulating those answers. You'll want to be able to come back and count the number of questions with missing answers. If an entire questionnaire is unusable, count in the "not usable" box on Form 15-2.

Compute totals at the bottom of each copy of the tabulation form, then add the totals from the copies of the form and record on Form 15-3.

Code a few questionnaires on Form 15-2 and tabulate them on Form 15-3 before you do all the questionnaires—just to be sure that you understand what you are doing.

Whether you tabulate the surveys manually or by computer you will do the same basic analyses. The computer will allow you to do additional analyses with ease. Forms 15-3 and 15-4 will guide manual analysis. (Worked examples 14-3S and 14-4S are very similar.) When using a computer, use Form 15-4 as a guide for the analyses that you need.

1. For each question, count the *frequency* with which each value appears, that is, the number of 1's, 2's, etc., circled for each. Also count the number of times the question was left blank.

Library _____

Sample Period _____

Form 15-2
Online Search Evaluation Tabulation (pg. 1)

#	Understanding						Thoroughness						Relevance						Amount					
	0	1	2	3	4	5	0	1	2	3	4	5	0	1	2	3	4	5	0	1	2	3	4	5
Page Total																								

Not usable: _____

2. Calculate the *percentage* of 1's, 2's, etc., for each item. Exclude from percentages the people who didn't answer the question.
3. Calculate the *average* score for the library. Again, exclude "missing" answers. (Note that for questions 8 and 9 an average would make no sense.)

Form 15-2
Online Search Evaluation Tabulation (pg. 2)

#	Currency 0 1 2 3 4 5	Time 0 1 2 3 4 5	Overall 0 1 2 3 4 5	Status U G F R S O	Purpose C R T CA M O
Page Total					

DISCUSSION

Users' assessment of their satisfaction with their online literature search depends on many factors, including the outcome of the search, the interaction with the search intermediary, the library as a whole, the cost of the search in terms of dollars and the amount of time invested by the patron, the patrons' past experience with searches, their knowledge of the literature and bibliographic searching, and the availability of the information they are looking for online.

Form 15-3
Online Search Evaluation Survey Worksheet (pg. 1)

1. Understanding (Compute totals from bottom of Form 15-2)

(1)	(2) Number	(3) Percent[1]	(4) (1) × (2)
1			
2			
3			
4			
5			
Total		100%	
No answer[2]			

Average (divide Total from column 4 by Total from column 2):____

[1]Enter these percentages on Form 15-4.
[2]Do not use this number in calculating percentages.

2. Thoroughness (Compute totals from bottom of Form 15-2)

(1)	(2) Number	(3) Percent[1]	(4) (1) × (2)
1			
2			
3			
4			
5			
Total		100%	
No answer[2]			

Average (divide Total from column 4 by Total from column 2):____

[1]Enter these percentages on Form 15-4.
[2]Do not use this number in calculating percentages.

3. Relevance (Compute totals from bottom of Form 15-2)

(1)	(2) Number	(3) Percent[1]	(4) (1) × (2)
1			
2			
3			
4			
5			
Total		100%	
No answer[2]			

Average (divide Total from column 4 by Total from column 2):____

[1]Enter these percentages on Form 15-4.
[2]Do not use this number in calculating percentages.

4. Amount (Compute totals from bottom of Form 15-2)

(1)	(2) Number	(3) Percent[1]	(4) (1) × (2)
1			
2			
3			
4			
5			
Total		100%	
No answer[2]			

Average (divide Total from column 4 by Total from column 2):____

[1]Enter these percentages on Form 15-4.
[2]Do not use this number in calculating percentages.

5. Currency (Compute totals from bottom of Form 15-2)

(1)	(2) Number	(3) Percent[1]	(4) (1) × (2)
1			
2			
3			
4			
5			
Total		100%	
No answer[2]			

Average (divide Total from column 4 by Total from column 2):____

[1]Enter these percentages on Form 15-4.
[2]Do not use this number in calculating percentages.

6. Time (Compute totals from bottom of Form 15-2)

(1)	(2) Number	(3) Percent[1]	(4) (1) × (2)
1			
2			
3			
4			
5			
Total		100%	
No answer[2]			

Average (divide Total from column 4 by Total from column 2):____

[1]Enter these percentages on Form 15-4.
[2]Do not use this number in calculating percentages.

Form 15-3
Online Search Evaluation Survey Worksheet (pg. 2)

7. Overall (Compute totals from bottom of Form 15-2)

(1)	(2) Number	(3) Percent[1]	(4) (1) × (2)
1			
2			
3			
4			
5			
Total		100%	
No answer[2]			

Average (divide Total from column 4
by Total from column 2):____

[1] Enter these percentages on Form 15-4.
[2] Do not use this number in calculating percentages.

8. Status of Respondents (Compute totals from bottom of Form 15-2)

Status	Number	Percent[1]
a. Undergraduates		
b. Graduate students		
c. Faculty		
d. Research staff		
e. Other staff		
f. Other		
Total		100%
No answer[2]		

[1] Enter these percentages on Form 15-4.
[2] Do not use this number in calculating percentages.

9. Purpose (Compute totals from bottom of Form 15-2)

Purpose	Number	Percent[1]
a. Course work		
b. Research		
c. Teaching		
d. Current awareness		
e. Mix of purposes		
f. Other		
Total		100%
No answer[2]		

[1] Enter these percentages on Form 15-4.
[2] Do not use this number in calculating percentages.

Form 15-4
Summary of Results of Online Satisfaction Survey

1. Number of questionnaires distributed:_____
2. Number of questionnaires returned and usable:_____
3. Response rate (Divide line 2 by line 1):_____

Measure ╲ Rank	1	2	3	4	5	Average
Understanding						
Thoroughness						
Relevance						
Amount						
Currency						
Time						
Overall						

Status of Respondents

Undergraduates	Graduate students	Faculty	Research staff	Other staff	Other	Total
						100%

# of responses _____   (Total, Table 8, Form 15-3)

Purpose

Course work	Research	Teaching	Current awareness	Mix of purposes	Other	Total
						100%

# of responses _____   (Total, Table 9, Form 15-3)

Some users will report success when a librarian might not, and vice versa. Some users will be unrealistically critical; some overly forgiving. However, users' self-reports of their satisfaction with online searches provides valuable information. The open-ended comments will help identify areas where improvement is needed.

The most important variable here is the patron's expectations of the search process and the product. The more the library can do to educate their users about the search process and product, the more likely the patrons are to be satisfied.

SAMPLE MATERIALS AVAILABILITY SURVEY REPORT

SPSS-PC+ was used for the analyses. The SPSS output was then edited in a word processor to produce the following report.

Materials Availability Survey, October, 198X

Questionnaires were distributed during 8.75 randomly selected hours during the week of October X. 619 questionnaires were distributed, for an average of 71 per hour; 368 were returned usable, for a response rate of 62%.

Surveyors were stationed near the entrance to the stacks and near the circulation service desk, in an effort to survey only people who were searching for materials on this library visit. Of the questionnaires returned, 282, or 77%, of the respondents reported that they were searching for materials.

Only people reporting that they were looking for materials are included in the analyses below.

STATUS OF
RESPONDENTS

	Frequency	Percent	Valid Percent	Cumulative Percent
undergraduates	80	28.4	28.6	28.6
graduate students	138	48.9	49.3	77.9
faculty	13	4.6	4.6	82.5
research staff	8	2.8	2.9	85.4
other staff	8	2.8	2.9	88.2
other	33	11.7	11.8	100.0
no answer	2	.7	Missing	
TOTAL	282	100.0	100.0	

Total number of materials searches reported: 492

MEAN FILL RATE (proportion of searches that are successful) by RESPONDENT
STATUS

	Mean	Standard Deviation	Cases
All Respondents	.63	.42	243
undergraduates	.64	.44	68
graduate students	.63	.42	124
faculty	.62	.42	10
research staff	.85	.22	8
other staff	.83	.40	6
other	.54	.41	27

NUMBER OF SEARCHES REPORTED BY RESPONDENTS (who said they were
searching for materials)

No. of Searches	No. of Respondents	Valid Percent	Cumulative Percent	Percent
1	112	39.7	45.9	45.9
2	69	24.5	28.3	74.2
3	29	10.3	11.9	86.1
4	18	6.4	7.4	93.4
5	14	5.0	5.7	99.2
6	1	.4	.4	99.6
7	1	.4	.4	100.0
no answer	38	13.5	Missing	
Total	282	100.0	100.0	

MEAN NUMBER OF SEARCHES BY RESPONDENT STATUS

All Respondents	2.02	1.25	243
undergraduates	1.98	1.31	68
graduate students	2.02	1.22	124
faculty	1.80	1.31	10
research staff	2.62	1.84	8
other staff	1.00	.00	6
other	2.22	1.05	27

WHAT WILL YOU USE THESE MATERIALS FOR? (PURPOSE)
Undergraduates who answered "research" were changed to "course work."

	Frequency	Percent	Valid Percent	Cumulative Percent
course work	73	25.9	27.2	27.2
teaching	5	1.8	1.9	29.1
research	111	39.4	41.4	70.5
current awareness	8	2.8	3.0	73.5
mix	56	19.9	20.9	94.4
other	15	5.3	5.6	100.0
no answer	14	5.0	Missing	
Total	282	100.0	100.0	

MEAN FILL RATE (proportion of successful searches) by RESPONDENT
(PURPOSE)

	Mean	Standard Deviation	Cases
course work	.58	.45	47
teaching	.62	.47	4
research	.67	.39	114
current awareness	.59	.41	8
mix of purposes	.62	.44	54
other	.78	.38	13

PURPOSE BY STATUS

			Status			
Purpose	Count Column %	Undergrad	Grad	Faculty	All Other	Row Total
course work	1	50 64.9%	21 16.0%	1 8.3%	1 2.2%	73 27.4%
teaching	2		4 3.1%			4 1.5%
research	3		73 55.7%	8 66.7%	30 65.2%	111 41.7%
current aware-ness	4	3 3.9%	4 3.1%		1 2.2%	8 3.0%
mix of purposes	5	20 26.0%	26 19.8%	3 25.0%	6 13.0%	55 20.7%
other	6	4 5.2%	3 2.3%		8 17.4%	15 5.6%
	Column Total	77 100%	131 100%	12 100%	46 100%	266 100.0%

Number of missing observations = 16

MEAN NUMBER OF SEARCHES BY RESPONDENT PURPOSE

	Mean	Standard Deviation	Cases
All Respondents	2.01	1.25	240
course work	1.74	1.20	47
teaching	2.25	1.50	4
research	1.99	1.26	114
current awareness	2.37	1.50	8
mix of purposes	2.31	1.28	54
other	1.69	.85	13

OVERALL, HOW SUCCESSFUL WERE YOU AT FINDING MATERIALS TODAY?

	Value	Frequency	Percent	Valid Percent	Cumulative Percent
Not at all	1	33	11.7	13.0	13.0
	2	12	4.3	4.7	17.8
	3	49	17.4	19.4	37.2
	4	45	16.0	17.8	54.9
Completely	5	114	40.4	45.1	100.0
No answer	.	29	10.3	Missing	
Total		282	100.0	100.0	

MEAN SUCCESS RATINGS BY RESPONDENT STATUS
(scale from 1 = "not at all" to 5 = "completely successful")

	Mean	Standard Deviation	Cases
All Respondents	3.76	1.40	252
undergraduates	3.65	1.51	70
graduate students	3.68	1.42	129
faculty	4.50	.79	12
research staff	4.37	.74	8
other staff	4.66	.81	6
other	3.74	1.31	27

MEAN SUCCESS RATINGS BY RESPONDENT PURPOSE
(scale from 1 = "not at all" to 5 = "completely successful")

	Mean	Standard Deviation	Cases
All Respondents	3.79	1.38	249
course work	3.57	1.65	49
teaching	4.7	.50	4
research	3.96	1.25	126
current awareness	3.50	1.51	8
mix of purposes	3.70	1.40	50
other	3.25	1.42	12

SAMPLE GENERAL SATISFACTION SURVEY REPORT

SPSS-PC+ was used for the analyses. The SPSS output was then edited in a word processor to produce the following report.

General Satisfaction Survey, October 198X

RESPONSE RATE

Questionnaires were given to everyone entering the library during 10.25 randomly distributed hours during the week of October X, 198X. A total of 550 questionnaires was distributed, for an average of 54 per hour. 391 were returned and usable, for a response rate of 71%.

Question 1: "What Did You Do in the Library Today? For Each Activity, Rate How Successful You Were" (on a scale from 1 to 5). (Zero indicates individual "Did Not Do Today.")

LOOKED FOR BOOKS OR PERIODICALS

	Value	Frequency	Percent	Valid Percent	Cumulative Percent
Not at all successful	1	22	5.6	11.9	11.9
	2	17	4.3	9.2	21.1
	3	36	9.2	19.5	40.5
	4	43	11.0	23.2	63.8
Completely successful	5	67	17.1	36.2	100.0
Did not do today	0	206	52.7	Missing	
Total		391	100.0	100.0	

Mean value: 3.62
Respondents who performed this activity: 185 (47.3%)

STUDIED

	Value	Frequency	Percent	Valid Percent	Cumulative Percent
Not at all successful	1	6	1.5	4.0	4.0
	2	12	3.1	7.9	11.9
	3	24	6.1	15.9	27.8
	4	49	12.5	32.5	60.3
Completely successful	5	60	15.3	39.7	100.0
Did not do today	0	240	61.4	Missing	
Total		391	100.0	100.0	

Mean value:4.0
Respondents who performed this activity: 151 (38.6%)

REVIEWED CURRENT LITERATURE

	Value	Frequency	Percent	Valid Percent	Cumulative Percent
Not at all successful	1	8	2.0	13.1	13.1
	2	6	1.5	9.8	23.0
	3	14	3.6	23.0	45.9
	4	23	5.9	37.7	83.6
Completely successful	5	10	2.6	16.4	100.0
Did not do today	0	330	84.4	Missing	
Total		391	100.0	100.0	

Mean value: 3.3
Respondents who performed this activity: 61 (15.6%)

DID A LITERATURE SEARCH

	Value	Frequency	Percent	Valid Percent	Cumulative Percent
Not at all successful	1	12	3.1	10.8	10.8
	2	9	2.3	8.1	18.9
	3	22	5.6	19.8	38.7
	4	31	7.9	27.9	66.7
Completely successful	5	37	9.5	33.3	100.0
Did not do today	0	280	71.6	Missing	
Total		391	100.0	100.0	

Mean value: 3.6
Respondents who performed this activity: 111 (28.4%)

ASKED A REFERENCE QUESTION

	Value	Frequency	Percent	Valid Percent	Cumulative Percent
Not at all successful	1	8	2.0	8.5	8.5
	2	4	1.0	4.3	12.8
	3	19	4.9	20.2	33.0
	4	20	5.1	21.3	54.3
Completely successful	5	43	11.0	45.7	100.0
Did not do today	0	297	76.0	Missing	
Total		391	100.0	100.0	

Mean value: 3.9
Respondents who performed this activity: 94 (24%)

BROWSED

	Value	Frequency	Percent	Valid Percent	Cumulative Percent
Not at all successful	1	4	1.0	7.7	7.7
	2	6	1.5	11.5	19.2
	3	13	3.3	25.0	44.2
	4	18	4.6	34.6	78.8
Completely successful	5	11	2.8	21.2	100.0
Did not do today	0	339	86.7	Missing	
Total		391	100.0	100.0	

Mean value: 3.5
Respondents who performed this activity: 52 (13.3%)

RETURNED BOOKS

Respondents who performed this activity: 32 (8%)

HOW EASY WAS THE LIBRARY TO USE TODAY?

	Value	Frequency	Percent	Valid Percent	Cumulative Percent
Not at all easy	1	9	2.3	2.5	2.5
	2	15	3.8	4.1	6.6
	3	68	17.4	18.7	25.3
	4	87	22.3	23.9	49.2
Very easy	5	185	47.3	50.8	100.0
No answer	.	27	6.9	Missing	
Total		391	100.0	100.0	

Mean value: 4.2

OVERALL, HOW SATISFIED ARE YOU WITH TODAY'S LIBRARY VISIT?

	Value	Frequency	Percent	Valid Percent	Cumulative Percent
Not at all satisfied	1	16	4.1	4.3	4.3
	2	9	2.3	2.4	6.7
	3	91	23.3	24.5	31.2
	4	109	27.9	29.3	60.5
Very satisfied	5	147	37.6	39.5	100.0
No answer	.	19	4.9	Missing	
Total		391	100.0	100.0	

Mean value: 4.0

TODAY'S VISIT WAS PRIMARILY IN SUPPORT OF...
(Undergraduates' answers of "research" were changed to "course work.")

	Value	Frequency	Percent	Valid Percent	Cumulative Percent
Course work	1	179	45.8	47.4	47.4
Current awareness	2	13	3.3	3.4	50.8
Research	3	113	28.9	29.9	80.7
Teaching	4	2	.5	.5	81.2
Mix of purposes	5	43	11.0	11.4	92.6
Other	6	28	7.2	7.4	100.0
No answer	.	13	3.3	Missing	
Total		391	100.0	100.0	

STATUS OF RESPONDENTS

	Value	Frequency	Percent	Valid Percent	Cumulative Percent
undergraduates	1	134	34.3	35.2	35.2
graduate students	2	190	48.6	49.9	85.0
faculty	3	13	3.3	3.4	88.5
research staff	4	13	3.3	3.4	91.9
other staff	5	6	1.5	1.6	93.4
other	6	25	6.4	6.6	100.0
no answer	.	10	2.6	Missing	
Total		391	100.0	100.0	

RESPONDENTS'
ACADEMIC FIELD

	Value	Frequency	Percent	Valid Percent	Cumulative Percent
humanities	1	25	6.4	6.6	6.6
science	2	27	6.9	7.2	13.8
social science	3	288	73.7	76.6	90.4
other	4	36	9.2	9.6	100.0
no answer	.	15	3.8	Missing	
Total		391	100.0	100.0	

Mean Ratings by User Groups

Means are the average rating given by respondents in that group. Cases indicate number of people in that group responding to the question.

Where applicable, only includes people who reported that they performed an activity.

Mean rating on success in LOOKED FOR BOOKS OR PERIODICALS by levels of STATUS

	Mean	Standard Deviation	Cases
Entire Population	3.61	1.36	183
1 undergraduates	3.56	1.39	48
2 graduate students	3.62	1.37	90
3 faculty	3.69	1.54	13
4 research staff	3.37	1.59	8
5 staff	3.60	1.94	5
6 other	3.78	.97	19

Mean rating on success in STUDIED by levels of STATUS

	Mean	Standard Deviation	Cases
Entire Population	3.93	1.11	148
1 undergraduates	3.92	1.00	67
2 graduate students	4.00	1.18	75
3 faculty	2.50	2.12	2
5 staff	3.00	.00	1
6 other	4.00	1.00	3

Mean rating on success in REVIEWED CURRENT LITERATURE by levels of STATUS

	Mean	Standard Deviation	Cases
Entire Population	3.28	1.23	59
1 undergraduates	3.29	1.30	24
2 graduate students	3.10	1.23	29
4 research staff	4.00	.00	1
6 other	4.20	.44	5

Mean rating on success in DID A LITERATURE SEARCH by levels of STATUS

	Mean	Standard Deviation	Cases
Entire Population	3.64	1.31	110
1 undergraduates	3.27	1.39	33
2 graduate students	3.73	1.24	56
3 faculty	5.00	.00	3
4 research staff	4.14	1.06	7
5 staff	1.00	.00	1
6 other	3.90	1.28	10

Mean rating on success in ASKED A REFERENCE QUESTION by levels of STATUS

	Mean	Standard Deviation	Cases
Entire Population	3.87	1.27	91
1 undergraduates	3.66	1.38	27
2 graduate students	4.02	1.19	44
3 faculty	5.00	.00	2
4 research staff	4.00	.81	4
5 staff	3.50	2.12	2
6 other	3.66	1.43	12

Mean rating on success in BROWSED by levels of STATUS

	Mean	Standard Deviation	Cases
Entire Population	3.49	1.18	51
1 undergraduates	3.73	1.24	19
2 graduate students	3.22	1.21	18
3 faculty	3.20	1.30	5
4 research staff	4.00	.00	2
5 staff	3.00	.00	1
6 other	3.66	1.21	6

Mean rating on HOW EASY WAS THE LIBRARY TO USE TODAY
by levels of STATUS

	Mean	Standard Deviation	Cases
Entire Population	4.16	1.01	360
1 undergraduates	4.19	.88	122
2 graduate students	4.09	1.13	183
3 faculty	4.33	1.07	12
4 research staff	4.23	1.01	13
5 staff	4.60	.54	5
6 other	4.40	.71	25

Mean rating on OVERALL SATISFACTION by levels of STATUS

	Mean	Standard Deviation	Cases
Entire Population	3.96	1.06	368
1 undergraduates	3.96	.93	130
2 graduate students	3.96	1.16	182
3 faculty	4.00	1.29	13
4 research staff	4.00	1.04	12
5 staff	3.50	1.22	6
6 other	4.08	.75	25

PROPORTION OF USERS WHO PERFORMED EACH ACTIVITY, BY ACADEMIC STATUS

	Undergrad	Grad	Faculty	Other	
LOOKED FOR BOOKS/PERIODICALS	48 35.8%	90 47.4%	13 100.0%	32 72.7%	183 48.0%
STUDIED	67 50.0%	75 39.5%	2 15.4%	4 9.1%	148 38.8%
REVIEWED CURRENT LIT	24 17.9%	29 15.3%		6 13.6%	59 15.5
DID LIT SEARCH	33 24.6%	56 29.5%	3 23.1%	18 40.9%	110 28.9%
ASKED REF QUESTION	27 20.1%	44 23.2%	2 15.4%	18 40.9%	91 23.9%
BROWSED	19 14.2%	18 9.5%	5 38.5%	9 20.5%	51 13.4%
RETURNED BOOKS	5 3.7%	17 8.9%	1 7.7%	6 13.6%	29 7.6%
Column	134 100%	190 100%	13 100%	44 100%	381

Number of missing observations = 10

ADDED EASY MEASURES

These suggested measures are in addition to those in Part 2 and the "Further Suggestions" under each measure. Some are new combinations of data collected for the measures in this manual; some are based on IPEDS data; some are based on data many libraries have available. They are intended to spur thinking and offer examples of ways of using data to reflect library performance. Definitions and instructions are not included; choose definitions and methods that are most useful for your library. Time periods may be whatever is useful: per year, per academic term, etc.

Materials Availability and Use

Ratio of circulation to attendance
Recalls and/or overdues per circulation
Circulation per volume in collection (circulation divided by collection size)
Circulation per volume added
Circulation per staff FTE
Circulation per public service staff FTE
Circulation per hour open
No. of reserves circulated
Reserve circulation as percent of total circulation
Recalls handled
Recalls as percent of total circulation
ILLs requested (for your users)
ILL requests received from other libraries
ILL requests filled for other libraries
Outgoing ILL success rate (ratio of requests filled to requests received)
Ratio of outgoing ILLs to incoming ILLs

Facilities and Library Uses

User seats per person in primary population served
Users present (Building Use) per person in primary population served
Attendance per hour open
Attendance per staff FTE
Attendance per professional staff FTE
Circulation per attendance
Attendance as percent of primary population served
Remote uses as percent of total use

Information Services

Ratio of reference transactions to attendance
Reference transactions per circulation
Online searches per year
Ratio of online searches to reference transactions

Other

Staff hours of formal group instruction
Students reached through formal group instruction per year
Students reached per staff hour of formal group instruction
Professional staff FTE per person in primary user population
Total staff FTE per person in primary user population
Volumes held per person in primary user population
Volumes added per person in primary user population

BLANK FORMS

The forms on the following pages may be copied and used as needed. Most can be used as they appear here, perhaps with minor changes such as the addition of your library name. Some may require some editing to suit local circumstances.

Form 1-1
General Satisfaction Survey

PLEASE HELP US IMPROVE LIBRARY SERVICE BY
ANSWERING A FEW QUESTIONS.

1. What did you do in the library today? For each, circle the number that best reflects how successful you were.

	Successful?					
	Did not do today	**Not at all**				**Completely**
Looked for books or periodicals	0	1	2	3	4	5
Studied	0	1	2	3	4	5
Reviewed current literature	0	1	2	3	4	5
Did a literature search (manual or computer)	0	1	2	3	4	5
Asked a reference question	0	1	2	3	4	5
Browsed	0	1	2	3	4	5
Returned books	0	1	2	3	4	5
Other (what?)_____	0	1	2	3	4	5

2. How easy was the library to use today? *(Circle one)*:

          1   2   3   4   5
Not at all easy   **Very easy**

Why? _____

3. Overall, how satisfied are you with today's library visit? *(Circle one)*:

          1   2   3   4   5
Not at all satisfied   **Very satisfied**

Why? _____

4. Today's visit was primarily in support of *(Check one)*:
___1. Course work   ___3. Teaching   ___5. A mix of several purposes
___2. Research   ___4. Current awareness   ___6. Other:_____

5. You are *(Check one)*:
___1. Undergraduate   ___3. Faculty   ___5. Other staff
___2. Graduate student ___4. Research staff   ___6. Other (what?)_____

6. Your field *(Check one)*:
___1. Humanities ___2. Sciences ___3. Social Sciences ___4. Other (What?)_____

OTHER COMMENTS? Please use back of form.

Form 1-2
General Satisfaction Survey
Tabulation (pg. 1)

#	Looked for books 0 1 2 3 4 5	Studied 0 1 2 3 4 5	Reviewed current literature 0 1 2 3 4 5	Did a literature search 0 1 2 3 4 5
Page Total				

Not Usable:

Form 1-2
General Satisfaction Survey
Tabulation (pg.2)

No.___of___

#	Asked a reference question						Browsed						Returned books[1]		Other					
	0	1	2	3	4	5	0	1	2	3	4	5	No	Yes	0	1	2	3	4	5
Page Total																				

[1] No Answer or "Did not do today" should be entered as "no"; responses 1 through 5 should be entered as "yes".

Form 1-2
General Satisfaction Survey
Tabulation (pg.3)

No. ___ of ___

#	Ease of Use					Satisfaction					Purpose						Status						Field			
	1	2	3	4	5	1	2	3	4	5	1	2	3	4	5	6	1	2	3	4	5	6	H	SS	S	O
Page Total																										

Form 1-3
General Satisfaction Survey Worksheet (pg. 1)

1. Number of questionnaires distributed: _____
2. Number of questionnaires returned and usable: _____ (Enter on Form 1-4)
RESPONSE RATE: _____ (Enter on Form 1-4)
     (Divide line 2 by line 1)

1. User Success in Specific Library Activities

Library Activity _____
(Fill in activity from Form 1-2 [e.g., Looked for Books or Periodicals], and compute totals from bottom of Form 1-2. One copy of this table should be completed for each library activity in question 1 of Form 1-1.)

(1) SUCCESS	(2) No.	(3) %	(4) No.	(5) $\%^1$	(6) $(1)\times(4)^2$
0 - Did not do today/No answer					
1 - Not at all successful					
2 - Mostly unsuccessful					
3 - Neither					
4 - Mostly successful					
5 - Completely successful					
Total		100%		100%	

Percent of respondents who performed this activity. (Divide column 4 Total by column 2 Total) _____ (to Form 1-4, line a).

Average (divide column 6 Total by column 4 Total): _____ (to Form 1-4, line b)
     [1]Percent of total, column 4.
     [2]Multiply the number in column 1 by number of responses in column 4.

Note: For the library activity "returned books," simply compute the % of respondents who reported that they returned books:

     # who returned books / total number of respondents

Enter percentage who returned books directly on Form 1-4.

Form 1-3
General Satisfaction Survey Worksheet (pg. 2)

2. Ease of Use (compute totals from bottom of Form 1-2)

(1) Ease of Use	(2) Number	(3) Percent[1]	(4) $(1) \times (2)$[2]
1 - Not at all easy			
2 - Not easy			
3 - Neither			
4 - Mostly easy			
5 - Very easy			
Total	[3]	100%	
6 - No answer[4]			

Average (divide column 4 Total by column 2 Total):_____

[1]Enter these percentages in Table 2, Form 1-4.
[2]Multiply the number in column 1 by number of responses in column 2.
[3]Enter this number in Table 2, Form 1-4.
[4]Do not use this number in calculating percentages.

3. Satisfaction with Library Visit (compute totals from bottom of Form 1-2)

(1) Satisfaction	(2) Number	(3) Percent[1]	(4) $(1) \times (2)$[2]
1 - Not at all satisfied			
2 - Not satisfied			
3 - Neither			
4 - Mostly satisfied			
5 - Very satisfied			
Total	[3]	100%	
6 - No answer[4]			

Average (divide column 4 Total by column 2 Total):_____

[1]Enter these percentages in Table 3, Form 1-4.
[2]Multiply the number in column 1 by number of responses in column 2.
[3]Enter this number in Table 3, Form 1-4.
[4]Do not use this number in calculating percentages.

Form 1-3
General Satisfaction Survey Worksheet (pg. 3)

4. Purpose (compute totals from bottom of Form 1-2)

(1) Purpose	(2) Number	(3) Percent[1]
a. Course work		
b. Research		
c. Teaching		
d. Current awareness		
e. Mix of several purposes		
f. Other		
Total	[2]	100%
g. No answer[3]		

[1]Enter these percentages in Table 4, Form 1-4.
[2]Enter this number in Table 4, Form 1-4.
[3]Do not use this number in calculating percentages.

5. Status of Respondents (compute totals from bottom of Form 1-2)

(1) Status	(2) Number	(3) Percent[1]
a. Undergraduates		
b. Graduate students		
c. Faculty		
d. Research staff		
e. Other staff		
f. Other		
Total	[2]	100%
g. No answer[3]		

[1]Enter these percentages in Table 5, Form 1-4.
[2]Enter this number in Table 5, Form 1-4.
[3]Do not use this number in calculating percentages.

Form 1-3
General Satisfaction Survey Worksheet (pg. 4)

6. Field of Study (compute totals from bottom of Form 1-2)

(1) Field	(2) Number	(3) Percent[1]
a. Humanities		
b. Sciences		
c. Social sciences		
d. Other		
Total	[2]	100%
g. No answer[3]		

[1]Enter these percentages in Table 6, Form 1-4.
[2]Enter this number in Table 6, Form 1-4.
[3]Do not use this number in calculating percentages.

No. of Questionnaires Returned and Usable: _____
Response rate: _____

Date of Survey: _____

Form 1-4
Summary of Results of General Satisfaction Survey (pg. 1)

Table 1. Summary of User Success Rates

(Enter percentages from column 5 of the tables in question 1, Form 1-3)

Success \ Activity	a. Looked for books or periodicals	b. Studied	c. Reviewed current literature	d. Did literature search	e. Asked a reference question	f. Browsed	g. Returned books	h. Other
a. % of respondents who performed this								
Of users who performed this activity, % who were (from Form 1-3, column 5):								
1 - Not at all successful								
2 - Mostly unsuccessful								
3 - Neither success nor unsuccessful								
4 - Mostly successful								
5 - Completely successful								
b. Average rating (from Form 1-3)								

Form 1-4
Summary of Results of General Satisfaction Survey (pg. 2)

Table 2. Ease of Use

(Enter the percentages from question 2, column 3, Form 1-3. Enter the average from the bottom of the table in question 2, Form 1-3.)

Not at all easy	Not easy	Neither easy nor difficult	Mostly easy	Very easy	Total	Average rating
					100%	

# of responses _____ (Total, column 2, Form 1-3)

Table 3. User Satisfaction with Library

(Enter the percentages from question 3, column 3, Form 1-3. Enter the average from the bottom of the table on question 3, Form 1-3.)

Not at all satisfied	Mostly dissatisfied	Neither satisfied nor dissatisfied	Mostly satisfied	Very satisfied	Total	Average
					100%	

# of responses _____ (Total, column 2, Form 1-3)

Table 4. Purpose (Enter the percentages from question 4, Form 1-3)

Course work	Research	Teaching	Current awareness	Mix of purpose	Other	Total
						100%

# of responses _____ (Total, column 2, Form 1-3)

Table 5. Status of Respondents (Enter the percentages from question 5, Form 1-3)

Undergraduates	Graduate students	Faculty	Research staff	Other staff	Other	Total
						100%

# of responses _____ (Total, column 2, Form 1-3)

Table 6. Field of Study (Enter the percentages from question 6, Form 1-3)

Humanities	Sciences	Social sciences	Other	Total
				100%

# of responses _____ (Total, column 2, Form 1-3)

Form 3-1
In-Library Materials Use

Library _____

Date _____

Use one tally sheet for each day. At designated times, collect and count the materials left for reshelving. Enter the time at the top of the form.

Area or Type of Material	Hour															Totals
Totals																

Form 5-1
Materials Availability Survey

DID YOU FIND IT?

PLEASE HELP US IMPROVE SERVICE by telling us whether you found the library materials you looked for today. Use this form as scratch paper while you look in the catalog and on the shelf.

Your status (check one):

_____1. Undergraduate   _____4. Research staff
_____2. Graduate student   _____5. Other staff
_____3. Faculty   _____6. Other (what?) _____

If you were NOT looking for library materials today, please check here _____ and stop. THANK YOU!

Author/Title/Journal/etc. (abbreviations are fine)	Call #	Found on shelf? CIRCLE
_____		Yes No
_____		Yes No
_____		Yes No
_____		Yes No
_____		Yes No

OVERALL, how <u>successful</u> were you at finding materials today?

        1   2   3   4   5
    Not at all   Completely successful

What will you use these materials for? Primarily:

_____1. Course work   _____4. Current awareness
_____2. Research   _____5. A mix of several purposes
_____3. Teaching   _____6. Other: _____

MORE ITEMS? COMMENTS? Use the back of this form. THANK YOU!

PLEASE DROP IN BOX AT EXIT AS YOU LEAVE.

Form 5-2
Materials Availability Survey
Tabulation

#	Status							Not Looking	# Found	# Not Found	Success					Uses					
	1	2	3	4	5	6					1	2	3	4	5	1	2	3	4	5	6
Page total																					

Cannot tab:

Library_____   Date_____

Form 5-3
Materials Availability Survey Worksheet

1 - Number of questionnaires distributed	
2 - Number of refusals	
3 - Total (1) + (2)	
4 - Number of questionnaires returned and usable	
5 - Response rate (Divide line 4 by line 3)	
6 - Number of respondents not searching for material (Total from "not looking" column, all copies of Form 5-2)	
7 - Number of questionnaires reporting searches (Subtract line 6 from line 4)	
8 - Number of items found (Total from "found" column, all copies of Form 5-2)	
9 - Number of items not found (Total from "not found" column, all copies of Form 5-2)	
10 - Total searches (Add lines 8 and 9)	
11 - Average number of searches per person looking for materials (Divide line 10 by line 7)	
12 - **Materials Availability Rate** (Divide line 8 by line 10 and enter on Form 5-4, line 1a)	
13 - Margin: plus or minus (from Table 5-1, using # from line 10; see instructions; enter on Form 5-1, line 1b)	

No. of Questionnaires Returned and Usable:_____   Date of Survey:_____
Response rate:_____

Form 5-4
Materials Availability Survey Summary (pg. 1)

1. Materials Availability Rate (from Form 5-3, line 12) (a)_____   + or – (b)_____
(from Form 5-3, line 13)

2. Status of respondents
(Totals from "status" column, all copies of Form 5-2)

Status	All respondents		Searchers[1] [optional]	
	Number	Percent	Number	Percent
Undergraduates				
Graduate students				
Faculty				
Research staff				
Other staff				
Other				
Total		100%		100%
No answer				

[1]Respondents who were searching for materials. "Optional": see instructions in text. From Form 5-2, count only respondents who did not check "not looking."

3. Overall user materials search success rate
(Totals from "success" columns, all copies of Form 5-2)

(1) Success	(2) Number	(3) Percent of line 6	(4) (1) × (2)[1]
1. Not at all successful			
2. Mostly unsuccessful			
3. Neither			
4. Mostly succesful			
5. Very successful			
6. Total		100%	
No answer[2]			

Average (divide column 4 Total by column 2 Total):____

[1]Multiply the number in column 1 by the number of responses in column 2.
[2]Do not use this number in calculating percentages.

Form 5-4
Materials Availability Survey Summary (pg. 2)

4. Uses of materials
   (Totals from "uses" columns, all copies of Form 5-2)

Uses of Material	Number	Percent
1. Course work		
2. Research		
3. Teaching		
4. Current awareness		
5. Mix of several purposes		
6. Other		
Total		100%
No answer		

Form 6-1
Requested Material Log

A # of Request	B Patron Name or Title of Request	C Date Request Made	D Date Request Arrives	E Date Patron Notified	F Delay Time (C–D)	G Delay Time (C–E)

Form 6-2
Requested Materials Delay

Delay	Number	Percentage
Canceled		
Total		

Form 6-3
Requested Materials Delay
Median Determination Worksheet

Delay	# of Requests	Cumulative Total

Form 10-1
Facilities Data Collection Form

Department: _____   Date: _____   ____ of ____

Directions: At sampling time, go quickly through the library and count the number of people using each of the following. *Use Rate is Number in Use divided by Number Available.*

OBSERVATIONS

Facilities	Number Available	Time:		Time:		Time:		Time:		Time:		Time:		Time:	
		# in Use	Use Rate*	# in Use	Use Rate	# in Use	Use Rate	# in Use	Use Rate	# in Use	Use Rate	# in Use	Use Rate	# in Use	Use Rate

*Divide # in Use by Number Available.

Form 10-2
Average Facilities Use Rate Summary

Average Facilities Use Rate = Average of All Observations

Facilities	Number Available	Average Facilities Use Rate

152

Form 11-1
Service Point Data Collection Form

Department: _____   Date: _____

_____ of _____

Directions: At sampling time, go quickly through the library and count the number of users at each of the following service points. Count both users being served and those waiting.

Service Points	Users									Average
	Time:	Time:	Time:	Time:	Time:	Time:	Time:	Time:	Time:	
Total										

Form 11-2
Service Point Summary

Service Points	Average Number of Users

Form 12-1
Building Use Data Collection Form

Library: _____

Date: _____ _____ of _____

Space	Number of Users											
	Time:	Time:	Time:	Time:	Time:	Time:	Time:	Time:	Time:	Time:	Time:	Time:
Total												

Average number of users: _____
(average totals)

Form 12-2
Building Use Summary

Space	Average Number of Users

Form 13-1
Reference Services Statistics
Daily Desk Reporting Form

Name:_____   Date:_____

May be a department, unit, or individual (as appropriate)

Hour	Reference	Total
8 – 9		
9 – 11		
11 – 1		
1 – 3		
3 – 5		
5 – 7		
7 – 9		
9 –		

Total:_____

Form 14-1
Reference Satisfaction Survey

PLEASE LET US KNOW HOW WE ARE DOING. Evaluate the *reference* service that you received today by circling one number on each of the following scales. Feel free to explain—use the back of the form.

If you were NOT asking a reference question today, please check here _____ and stop. Thank you.

1. *Relevance* of information provided:

> Not relevant   1   2   3   4   5   Very relevant

2. Satisfaction with the *amount* of information provided:

> Not satisfied   1   2   3   4   5   Very satisfied
> (too little, too much)   (the right amount)

3. *Completeness* of the answer that you received:

> Not complete   1   2   3   4   5   Very complete

4. *Helpfulness* of staff:

> Not helpful   1   2   3   4   5   Extraordinarily helpful

5. Overall, how *satisfied* are you?

> Not satisfied   1   2   3   4   5   Extremely satisfied

Why? _____

_____

6. You are:

> _____ 1. Undergraduate   _____ 4. Research staff
> _____ 2. Graduate student   _____ 5. Other staff
> _____ 3. Faculty   _____ 6. Other?_____

7. What will you use this information for?

> _____ 1. Course work   _____ 4. Current awareness
> _____ 2. Research   _____ 5. Mix of several purposes
> _____ 3. Teaching   _____ 6. Other?_____

THANK YOU! Please leave this questionnaire in the box.

USE BACK OF PAGE FOR ANY ADDITIONAL COMMENTS.

Library_____

No. ____ of ____

Sample Period ____

Form 14-2
Reference Satisfaction Survey Tabulation

#	Relevance					Amount					Completeness					Helpfulness					Overall					Status				Purpose					
	1	2	3	4	5	1	2	3	4	5	1	2	3	4	5	1	2	3	4	5	1	2	3	4	5	U	G	F	R	S	O	C	R	T	CA	M	O

Page Total

Not usable:

Form 14-3
Reference Satisfaction Survey Worksheet (pg. 1)

1. Relevance (Compute totals from bottom of Form 14-2)

(1)	(2) Number	(3) Percent[1]	(4) (1) × (2)
1			
2			
3			
4			
5			
Total		100%	
No answer[2]			

Average (divide Total from column 4 by Total from column 2):____

[1]Enter these percentages on Form 14-4.
[2]Do not use this number in calculating percentages.

2. Amount (Compute totals from bottom of Form 14-2)

(1)	(2) Number	(3) Percent[1]	(4) (1) × (2)
1			
2			
3			
4			
5			
Total		100%	
No answer[2]			

Average (divide Total from column 4 by Total from column 2):____

[1]Enter these percentages on Form 14-4.
[2]Do not use this number in calculating percentages.

3. Completeness (Compute totals from bottom of Form 14-2)

(1)	(2) Number	(3) Percent[1]	(4) (1) × (2)
1			
2			
3			
4			
5			
Total		100%	
No answer[2]			

Average (divide Total from column 4 by Total from column 2):____

[1]Enter these percentages on Form 14-4.
[2]Do not use this number in calculating percentages.

4. Helpfulness (Compute totals from bottom of Form 14-2)

(1)	(2) Number	(3) Percent[1]	(4) (1) × (2)
1			
2			
3			
4			
5			
Total		100%	
No answer[2]			

Average (divide Total from column 4 by Total from column 2):____

[1]Enter these percentages on Form 14-4.
[2]Do not use this number in calculating percentages.

Form 14-3
Reference Satisfaction Survey Worksheet (pg. 2)

5. Overall (Compute totals from bottom of Form 14-2)

(1)	(2) Number	(3) Percent[1]	(4) (1) × (2)
1			
2			
3			
4			
5			
Total		100%	
No answer[2]			

Average(divideTotal from column 4 by Total from column 2):____

[1]Enter these percentages on Form 14-4.
[2]Do not use this number in calculating percentages.

6. Status of Respondents (Compute totals from bottom of Form 14-2)

Status	Number	Percent[1]
1. Undergraduates		
2. Graduate students		
3. Faculty		
4. Research staff		
5. Other staff		
6. Other		
Total		100%
No answer[2]		

[1]Enter these percentages on Form 14-4.
[2]Do not use this number in calculating percentages.

7. Purpose (Compute totals from bottom of Form 14-2)

Purpose	Number	Percent[1]
1. Course work		
2. Research		
3. Teaching		
4. Current awareness		
5. Mix of purpose		
6. Other		
Total		100%
No answer[2]		

[1]Enter these percentages on Form 14-4.
[2]Do not use this number in calculating percentages.

Form 14-4
Summary of Results of Reference Satisfaction Survey

1. Number of questionnaires distributed:_____
2. Number of questionnaires returned and usable:_____
3. Response rate:_____
   (Divide line 2 by line 1)
4. Number of respondents not asking for reference assistance:_____
5. Number of questionnaires reporting on reference satisfaction:_____

Measure \ Rank	1	2	3	4	5	Average
Relevance						
Amount						
Completeness						
Helpfulness						
Overall						

Status of Respondents

Undergraduates	Graduate students	Faculty	Research staff	Other staff	Other	Total
						100%

# of responses _____ (Total, Table 6, Form 14-3)

Purpose

Course work	Research	Teaching	Current awareness	Mix of purposes	Other	Total
						100%

# of responses _____ (Total, Table 7, Form 14-3)

Form 15-1
Online Search Evaluation

PLEASE LET US KNOW HOW WE ARE DOING. Please indicate your satisfaction with the following aspects of your *online search* by CIRCLING a number on each of the following scales.

How satisfied are you with:

1. Searcher's <u>understanding</u> of your search request (main concept identified in developing the search strategy)?

    Not satisfied   1   2   3   4   5   Very satisfied

2. *<u>Thoroughness</u>* of the searcher in selecting appropriate database(s) and using relevant terms of phrases to retrieve references?

    Not satisfied   1   2   3   4   5   Very satisfied

3. *<u>Relevance</u>* of information provided?

    Not satisfied   1   2   3   4   5   Very satisfied

4. *<u>Amount</u>* of information provided (from your knowledge of the amount available in published sources)?

    Not satisfied   1   2   3   4   5   Very satisfied
    (too little, too much)   (the right amount)

    If not satisfied, please check: _____ Too little _____ Too much

5. *<u>Currency</u>* (up-to-dateness) of the information?

    Not satisfied   1   2   3   4   5   Very satisfied

6. *<u>Time</u>* taken to provide bibliography?

    Not satisfied   1   2   3   4   5   Very satisfied

7. Overall, how *<u>satisfied</u>* are you with the online search?

    Not satisfied   1   2   3   4   5   Very satisfied
    Why? _____

8. You are:

    _____ 1. Undergraduate   _____ 3. Faculty   _____ 5. Other staff
    _____ 2. Graduate student   _____ 4. Research staff   _____ 6. Other ?_____

9. What will you use this information for?

    _____ 1. Course work   _____ 3. Teaching   _____ 5. Several purposes
    _____ 2. Research   _____ 4. Current awareness   _____ 6. Other ?_____

Feel free to explain; please use the back of the page.

Library _____   No.___ of___
Sample Period _____

Form 15-2
Online Search Evaluation Tabulation (pg. 1)

#	Understanding						Thoroughness						Relevance						Amount					
	0	1	2	3	4	5	0	1	2	3	4	5	0	1	2	3	4	5	0	1	2	3	4	5
Page Total																								

Not usable: [   ]

Form 15-2
Online Search Evaluation Tabulation (pg. 2)

#	Currency						Time						Overall						Status						Purpose						
	0	1	2	3	4	5	0	1	2	3	4	5	0	1	2	3	4	5	U	G	F	R	S	O	C	R	T	CA	M	O
Page Total																														

Form 15-3
Online Search Evaluation Survey Worksheet (pg. 1)

1. Understanding (Compute totals from bottom of Form 15-2)

(1)	(2) Number	(3) Percent[1]	(4) (1) × (2)
1			
2			
3			
4			
5			
Total		100%	
6–No answer[2]			

Average (divide Total from column 4 by Total from column 2):____

[1]Enter these percentages on Form 15-4.
[2]Do not use this number in calculating percentages.

2. Thoroughness (Compute totals from bottom of Form 15-2)

(1)	(2) Number	(3) Percent[1]	(4) (1) × (2)
1			
2			
3			
4			
5			
Total		100%	
6–No answer[2]			

Average (divide Total from column 4 by Total from column 2):____

[1]Enter these percentages on Form 15-4.
[2]Do not use this number in calculating percentages.

3. Relevance (Compute totals from bottom of Form 15-2)

(1)	(2) Number	(3) Percent[1]	(4) (1) × (2)
1			
2			
3			
4			
5			
Total		100%	
6–No answer[2]			

Average (divide Total from column 4 by Total from column 2):____

[1]Enter these percentages on Form 15-4.
[2]Do not use this number in calculating percentages.

4. Amount (Compute totals from bottom of Form 15-2)

(1)	(2) Number	(3) Percent[1]	(4) (1) × (2)
1			
2			
3			
4			
5			
Total		100%	
6–No answer[2]			

Average (divide Total from column 4 by Total from column 2):____

[1]Enter these percentages on Form 15-4.
[2]Do not use this number in calculating percentages.

Form 15-3
Online Search Evaluation Survey Worksheet (pg. 2)

5. Currency (Compute totals from bottom of Form 15-2)

(1)	(2) Number	(3) Percent[1]	(4) (1) × (2)
1			
2			
3			
4			
5			
Total		100%	
6–No answer[2]			

Average (divide Total from column 4
by Total from column 2):____

[1]Enter these percentages on Form 15-4.
[2]Do not use this number in calculating percentages.

6.   Time (Compute totals from bottom of Form 15-2)

(1)	(2) Number	(3) Percent[1]	(4) (1) × (2)
1			
2			
3			
4			
5			
Total		100%	
6–No answer[2]			

Average (divide Total from column 4
by Total from column 2):____

[1]Enter these percentages on Form 15-4.
[2]Do not use this number in calculating percentages.

Form 15-3
Online Search Evaluation Survey Worksheet (pg. 3)

7. Overall (Compute totals from bottom of Form 15-2)

(1)	(2) Number	(3) Percent[1]	(4) (1) × (2)
1			
2			
3			
4			
5			
Total		100%	
No answer[2]		████	

Average (divide Total from column 4
by Total from column 2): ____

[1]Enter these percentages on Form 15-4.
[2]Do not use this number in calculating percentages.

8. Status of Respondents (Compute totals from bottom of Form 15-2)

Status	Number	Percent[1]
a. Undergraduates		
b. Graduate students		
c. Faculty		
d. Research staff		
e. Other staff		
f. Other		
Total		100%
No answer[2]		████

[1]Enter these percentages on Form 15-4.
[2]Do not use this number in calculating percentages.

Form 15-3
Online Search Evaluation Survey Worksheet (pg. 4)

9. Purpose (Compute totals from bottom of Form 15-2)

Purpose	Number	Percent[1]
a. Course work		
b. Research		
c. Teaching		
d. Current awareness		
e. Mix of purposes		
f. Other		
Total		100%
No answer[2]		

[1]Enter these percentages on Form 15-4.
[2]Do not use this number in calculating percentages.

Form 15-4
Summary of Results of Online Satisfaction Survey

1. Number of questionnaires distributed:_____
2. Number of questionnaires returned and usable:_____
3. Response rate (Divide line 2 by line 1):_____

Measure \ Rank	1	2	3	4	5	Average
Understanding						
Thoroughness						
Relevance						
Amount						
Currency						
Time						
Overall						

Status of Respondents

Undergraduates	Graduate students	Faculty	Research staff	Other staff	Other	Total
						100%

# of responses _____ (Total, Table 8, Form 15-3)

Purpose

Course work	Research	Teaching	Current awareness	Mix of purposes	Other	Total
						100%

# of responses _____ (Total, Table 9, Form 15-3)

GLOSSARY

(Measures described in Part 2 are preceded by an asterisk.)

*Attendance: Number of user visits to the library.

*Building Use: Average number of people in the library at any one time.

*Circulation: Number of items charged out for use, usually (though not always) outside the library. Includes initial charges and renewals, general collection, and reserves.

Confidence interval: Range of values within which a population parameter is estimated to lie.

Facilities: Space and equipment to be used (usually) in conjunction with the library's materials.

*Facilities Use Rate: The proportion of time, on average, that a facility is busy.

*General Satisfaction: Users' self-reports of success on each of several possible library activities, ease of use of the library, overall satisfaction with library visit.

*In-Library Materials Use: The number of items used in the library but not charged out.

*Library Uses: Number of user visits to the library. Number of people entering the library, including people attending activities, meetings, and those requiring no staff services.

Margin of error: *See* Sampling error.

*Materials Availability: The proportion of user searches for library materials that are successful at the time of the user's visit.

Materials provision: The provision of information materials, regardless of format, from within the collection or from other sources.

Mean: Average.

Median: The value at which half of the cases are above and half of the cases are below.

*Online Search Evaluation: Users' self-reports of satisfaction with the performance of the search intermediary and the search product, and overall satisfaction with the online search.

Outcomes: The effect of the outputs from the library on the larger environment, usually considered as benefits or impacts, e.g., the degree to which library use affects students' learning.

Outputs: The products and services created by the organization, many of which are used by library patrons, e.g., use of materials or online catalogs, answers to reference questions, etc.

Random sample: Sample in which every member of the larger population has an equal chance of being chosen for the sample.

*Reference Satisfaction: Users' evaluation of the outcome of reference transactions, the service experience, and overall satisfaction with the reference service.

*Reference Transaction: An information contact that involves the knowledge, use, recommendations, interpretation, or instruction in the use of one or more information sources by a member of the library staff.

Reliability: The quality of measurement such that the same results would be achieved from repeated measures of the same phenomenon.

*Remote Uses: Library uses for which the user does not come to the library, such as use of document delivery services, access to library catalogs or other online databases maintained by the library from terminals outside the library, or telephone, e-mail, or fax requests for materials or services.

*Requested Materials Delay: The length of time users must wait for requested material. This may be computed as the proportion of materials requested that are available within x number of days, or as median number of days required to receive requested materials.

Sample: A subset of cases used to represent a larger group or population.

Sampling error: The possible difference between the estimate derived from the sample and the true value for the entire population.

Service point: Staffed public service sites, for example, circulation, reference, and information desks.

*Service point use: The average number of users at a library service point.

*Total Materials Use: Total number of uses of library materials; sum of circulation and in-library materials use.

*Total Uses: Total uses of the library, in person and remote; sum of attendance and remote uses.

Validity: The characteristic of measures that accurately reflect what they are intended to measure.

BIBLIOGRAPHY

Altman, Ellen, Ernest R. DeProspo, Philip M. Clark, and Ellen Connor Clark. *A Data Gathering and Instructional Manual for Performance Measures in Public Libraries.* Chicago: Celadon Press, 1976.

American Library Association. Association of College and Research Libraries. Bibliographic Instruction Section. *Evaluating Bibliographic Instruction: A Handbook.* Chicago: American Library Association, 1983.

American Library Association. Association of College and Research Libraries. Standards and Accreditation Committee. "Guidelines for Extended Campus Library Services." *College and Research Libraries News* 43, no. 3 (1982): 86–88.

American Library Association. Association of College and Research Libraries. "Standards for College Libraries, 1986." *College and Research Libraries News* 47, no. 3 (1986): 189-99.

American Library Association. Association of College and Research Libraries. "Standards for University Libraries." *College and Research Libraries News* 40, no. 2 (1979): 101– 10.

American Library Association. Association of College and Research Libraries. ULS University Library Standards Review Committee. "Standards for University Libraries: Evaluation of Performance." *College and Research Libraries News* 50, no. 8 (1989): 679–91.

American Library Association. Library Administration and Management Association. Library Research Round Table. Reference and Adult Services Division. *Library Effectiveness: A State of the Art: Papers from a 1980 ALA Preconference.* Chicago: American Library Association, 1980.

Association of Research Libraries. *Planning for Management Statistics in ARL Libraries.* SPEC Kit #134. Washington, D.C.: Association of Research Libraries, 1987.

Association of Reasearch Libraries. *User Surveys.* SPEC Kit #148. Washington, D.C.: Association of Research Libraries.

Auster, Ethel. " User Satisfaction with the Online Negotiation Interview: Contemporary Concern in Traditional Perspective." *RQ* 23, no. 1 (1983): 47-59.

Auster, Ethel J., and Stephen B. Lawton. "Search Interview Techniques and Information Gain as Antecedents of User Satisfaction with Online Bibliographic Retrieval." *Journal of the American Society for Information Science* 35, no. 2 (1984): 90-103.

Aversa, Elizabeth. "Organizational Effectiveness in Libraries: A Review and Some Suggestions." *Drexel Library Quarterly* 17, no. 2 (1981): 27-45.

Babbie, Earl. *The Practice of Social Research.* 5th ed. Belmont, Calif.: Wadsworth Publishing Corp., 1989.

Babbie, Earl R. *Survey Research Methods.* Belmont, Calif.: Wadsworth Publishing Corp., 1973.

Balay, Robert, and Christine Andrew. "Use of the Reference Service in a Large Academic Library." *College and Research Libraries* 36, no. 1 (1975): 9–26.

Barreau, Deborah. "Using Performance Measures to Implement an Online Catalog." *Library Resources and Technical Services* 32, no. 4 (1988): 312-22.

Benham, Frances, and Ronald R. Powell. *Success in Answering Reference Questions: Two Studies.* Metuchen, N.J.: Scarecrow Press, 1987.

Blood, Richard W. *Evaluation of Online Searches.* ERIC Document ED227859. Washington, D.C.: ERIC, 1981.

Blood, Richard W. "Evaluation of Online Searches." *RQ* 22, no. 3 (1983): 266–77.

Bommer, Michael R. W., and Ronald W. Chorba. *Decision Making for Library Management.* White Plains, N.Y.: Knowledge Industry Publications, 1982.

Bookstein, Abraham. "How to Sample Badly." *Library Quarterly* 44, no. 2 (1974): 124–32.

Brittain, J. Michael. "Pitfalls of User Research, and Some Neglected Areas." *Social Science Information Studies* 2, no. 3 (1982): 139–48.

Broadus, Robert N. "Use Studies of Library Collections." *Library Resources and Technical Services* 24, no. 4 (1980): 317–24.

Brudenall, John. "Client Assessment of Reference Services." *Australian Library Journal* 25, no. 14 (1976): 367–69.

Buckland, Michael K. *Book Availability and the Library User.* New York: Pergamon Press, 1975.

Buckland, Michael K. *Library Services in Theory and Context.* 2d ed. Oxford: Pergamon Press, 1988.

Bunge, Charles. "Factors Related to Reference Question Answering Success: The Development of a Data-Gathering Form." *RQ* 24, no. 4 (1985): 482-86.

Bunge, Charles A. "Approaches to the Evaluation of Library Reference Services." In *Evaluation and Scientific Management of Libraries and Information Centres,* ed. F. W. Lancaster and C. W. Cleverdon, 41–71. Leyden: Noordhoff, 1977.

Bunge, Charles A., and Marjorie E. Murfin. "Reference Questions—Data from the Field." *RQ* 27, no. 1 (1987): 15–18.

Burns, Robert W., Jr. "Library Use as a Performance Measure: Its Background and Rationale." *Journal of Academic Librarianship* 4, no. 1 (1978): 4-11.

Cameron, Kim S., and David A. Whetten. "Some Conclusions about Organizational Effectiveness." In *Organizational Effectiveness: A Comparison of Multiple Models,* ed. Kim S. Cameron and David A. Whetten, 261–75. New York: Academic Press, 1983.

Casserly, Mary F. "Academic Library Regional Accreditation." *College and Research Libraries* 47, no. 1 (1986): 38–47.

Center for Education Statistics. *Library Statistics of Colleges and Universities, 1985.* Chicago: Association of College and Research Libraries, American Library Association, 1987.

Centre for Interfirm Comparison. *Inter-Library Comparisons in Academic Libraries.* British Library Research and Development Reports, no. 5763. Boston Spa, England: British Library Lending Division, 1984.

Childers, Thomas, and Nancy A. Van House. "Dimensions of Public Library Effectiveness." *Library and Information Science Research* 11, no. 4 (Dec./Jan. 1989/90): 273–301.

Christiansen, Dorothy E., C. Roger Davis, and Jutta Reed-Scott. "Guide to Collection Evaluation through Use and User Studies." *Library Resources and Technical Services* 27, no. 4 (1983): 432-40.

Ciliberti, Anne C. "The Development and Methodological Study of an Instrument for Measuring Material Availability in Libraries." New Brunswick, N.J.: Rutgers University Ph.D. diss., 1985.

Ciliberti, Anne C., and others. "Material Availability: A Study of Academic Library Performance." *College and Research Libraries* 48, no. 6 (1987): 513–27.

Ciucki, Marcella. "Recording of Reference/Information Service Activities: A Study of Forms Currently Used." *RQ* 16, no. 4 (1977): 273–322.

Crews, Kenneth D. "The Accuracy of Reference Service: Variables for Research and Implementation." *Library and Information Science Research* 10, no. 3 (1988): 331–55.

Cronin, Blaise. "Taking the Measure of Service." *ASLIB Proceedings* 34, no. 6/7 (1982): 273–94.

Cronin, Mary J. *Performance Measurement for Public Services in Academic and Research Libraries.* Washington, D.C.: Association of Research Libraries, 1985.

Daval, Nicola, and Celeste Feather. *ARL Statistics, 1987–1988.* Washington, D.C.: Association of Research Libraries, 1989.

D'Elia, George. "Materials Availability Fill Rates: Additional Data Addressing the Question of the Usefulness of the Measures." *Public Libraries* 27, no. 1 (1988b): 15–23.

D'Elia, George. "Materials Availability Fill Rates—Useful Measures of Library Performance?" *Public Libraries* 24, no. 3 (1985): 106–11.

D'Elia, George. "A Response to Van House." *Public Libraries* 27, no. 1 (1988a): 28–31.

D'Elia, George, and Carla Hutkins. "Faculty Use for Document Delivery Services: The Results of a Survey." *Journal of Academic Librarianship* 12, no. 2 (1984): 69–74.

D'Elia, George, and Sandra Walsh. "User Satisfaction with Library Service—A Measure of Public Library Performance?" *Library Quarterly* 53, no. 2 (1983): 109–33.

De Prospo, Ernest, Ellen Altman, and Kenneth E. Beasley. *Performance Measures for Public Libraries.* Chicago: American Library Association, 1973.

Dervin, Brenda, and Kathleen Clark. *ASQ: Asking Significant Questions: Alternative Tools for Information Need and Accountability Assessments by Libraries.* Belmont, Calif.: Peninsula Library System for the California State Library, 1987.

Dervin, Brenda, and Michael Nilan. "Information Needs and Uses." In *Annual Review of Information Science and Technology,* ed. Martha E. Williams, vol. 21, 3–33. White Plains, N.Y.: Knowledge Industry Publications, Inc., 1986.

Drott, Carl. "Random Sampling: A Tool for Library Research." *College and Research Libraries* 30, no. 2 (1969): 119–25.

Du Mont, Rosemary Ruhig. "A Conceptual Basis for Library Effectiveness." *College and Research Libraries* 41, no. 2 (1980): 103–11.

Du Mont, Rosemary Ruhig, and Paul F. Du Mont. "Assessing the Effectiveness of Library Service." Occasional Papers #152. Urbana-Champaign: University of Illinois Graduate School of Library and Information Science, 1981.

Du Mont, Rosemary Ruhig, and Paul F. Du Mont. "Measuring Library Effectiveness: A Review and an Assessment." In *Advances in Librarianship,* ed. Michael H. Harris, vol. 9, 103–41. New York: Academic Press, 1979.

Emerson, Katherine. 1974. "Symposium on Measurement of Reference." *RQ* 14, no. 1 (1974): 7–19.

Evans, Edward, Harold Borko, and Patricia Ferguson. 1972. "Review of Criteria Used to Measure Library Effectiveness." *Bulletin of the Medical Library Association* 60, no. 1 (1972): 102–10.

Fidel, Raya. "What Is Missing in Research about Online Searching Behavior." *Canadian Journal of Information Science* 12, no. 3/4 (1987): 54–61.

Ford, Geoffrey, ed. *User Studies: An Introductory Guide and Select Bibliography.* Sheffield, England: Centre for Research on User Studies, University of Sheffield, 1977.

Frost, William J. *College Library Instruction/College Instruction: A Review of the Literature.* ERIC Document ED 167131. Washington, D.C.: ERIC. 1978.

Goodall, Deborah. "Performance Measurement: A Historical Perspective." *Journal of Librarianship* 20, no. 2 (1988): 128–44.

Goodell, John S. *Libraries and Work Sampling.* Littleton, Colo.: Libraries Unlimited, 1975.

Graham, Elaine, Irene Lovas, and Virginia Flack. *Health Professionals' Use of Documents Obtained through the Regional Library Network*. Los Angeles: Pacific Southwest Regional Medical Library Service, 1988.

Halperin, Michael. "Cluster Sampling Reference Transactions." *RQ* 18, no. 4 (1978): 328–33.

Halperin, Michael. "Reference Question Sampling." *RQ* 14, no. 1 (1974): 20–23.

Hamburg, Morris, Richard C. Clelland, Michael R. W. Bommer, Leonard E. Ramist, and Ronald M. Whitfield. *Library Planning and Decision-Making Systems*. Cambridge, Mass.: MIT Press, 1974.

Hernon, Peter. "Utility Measures, Not Performance Measures, for Library Reference Service?" *RQ* 27, no. 4 (1987): 449–59.

Hernon, Peter, with Pat K. Bryant. *Statistics for Library Decision-Making: A Handbook*. Norwood, N.J.: Ablex Publishing, 1989.

Hernon, Peter, and Charles R. McClure. *Unobtrusive Testing and Library Reference Service*. Norwood, N.J.: Ablex Publishing, 1987.

Hernon, Peter, and John V. Richardson. *Microcomputer Software for Performing Statistical Analyses: A Handbook Supporting Library Decision-Making*. Norwood, N.J.: Ablex Publishing, 1988.

Hilchey, Susan E., and Jitka M. Hurych. "User Satisfaction or User Acceptance? Statistical Evaluation of an Online Reference Service." *RQ* 24, no. 4 (1985): 452–59.

Hoover, Ryan E. "Patron Appraisal of Computer-Aided On-Line Bibliographic Retrieval Services." *Journal of Library Automation* 9, no. 4 (1976): 335–50.

Jackson, William J. "Staff Selection and Training for Quality Online Searching." *RQ* 22, no. 1 (1982): 48–54.

Kania, Antoinette. "Academic Library Standards and Performance Measures." *College and Research Libraries* 49, no. 1 (1988): 16–23.

Kantor, Paul B. "Availability Analysis." *Journal of the American Society for Information Science* 27, no. 6 (1976b): 311–19.

Kantor, Paul B. "Evaluation of and Feedback in Information Storage and Retrieval Systems." In *Annual Review of Information Science and Technology*, ed. Martha E. Williams, vol. 17, 99–120. White Plains, N.Y.: Knowledge Industry Publications, 1982.

Kantor, Paul B. "The Library as an Information Utility in the University Context: Evolution and Measurement of Service." *Journal of the American Society for Information Science* 27, no. 2 (1976a): 100–12.

Kantor, Paul B. *Objective Performance Measures for Academic and Research Libraries*. Washington, D.C.: Association of Research Libraries, 1984.

Kantor, Paul B. "Quantitative Evaluation of the Reference Process." *RQ* 21, no. 1 (1981): 43–52.

Kantor, Paul B. "Vitality: An Indirect Measure of Relevance." *Collection Management* 2, no. 1 (1978): 83–95.

Katzer, Jeffrey. "The Evaluation of Libraries: Considerations from a Research Perspective." *Drexel Library Quarterly* 13, no. 3 (1977): 84–101.

Kent, Allen, and others. *Use of Library Materials: The University of Pittsburgh Study*. New York: Marcel Dekker, 1979.

Kesselman, Martin, and Sarah Barbara Watstein. "The Measurement of Reference and Information Services." *Journal of Academic Librarianship* 13, no. 1 (1987): 25–30.

Kingsley, Marcia. "A Closer Look at the Hobgoblin: Users' Satisfaction with Computerized Literature Searches." *North Carolina Libraries* 40, no. 1 (1982): 37–41.

Klaus, Peter G. "Quality Epiphenomenon: The Conceptual Understanding of Quality in Face-to-Face Service Encounters." In *The Service Encounter: Managing Employee/Customer Interaction in Service Businesses*, ed. John A. Czepiel, Michael R.

Solomon, and Carol F. Surprenant, 17–33. Lexington, Mass.: Lexington Books, 1985.

Knapp, Patricia B. *The Montieth College Library Experiment.* Metuchen, N.J.: Scarecrow Press, 1966.

Kolner, Stuart J., and Eric C. Welch. "The Book Availability Study as an Objective Measure of Performance in a Health Sciences Library." *Bulletin of the Medical Library Association* 73, no. 2 (1985): 121–31.

Krikelas, James. "Information-Seeking Behavior: Patterns and Concepts." *Drexel Library Quarterly* 19, no. 4 (1983): 5–20.

Lancaster, F. W. "Evaluating Collections by Their Use." *Collection Management* 4, no. 1/2 (1982): 15–43.

Lancaster, F. W. *If You Want to Evaluate Your Library....* Champaign: University of Illinois Graduate School of Library and Information Science. 1988.

Lancaster, F. W. *The Measurement and Evaluation of Library Services.* Washington, D.C.: Information Resources Press, 1977.

Loveday, Anthony J. "Statistics for Management and Trend Analysis: A SCONUL Experiment." *IFLA Journal* 14, no. 4 (1988): 334–42.

Lynch, Beverly P., ed. *Standards for University Libraries.* The Hague: IFLA Section of University Libraries and Other General Research Libraries, 1986.

Mansbridge, John. "Availability Studies in Libraries." *Library and Information Science Research* 8, no. 4 (1986): 299–314.

Martyn, John, and F. Wilfrid Lancaster. *Investigative Methods in Library and Information Science.* Washington, D.C.: Information Resources Press, 1981.

Mason, Richard O., and E. Burton Swanson, eds. 1981. *Measurement for Management Decision.* Reading, Mass.: Addison-Wesley, 1981.

McClure, Charles R. "Management Information for Library Decision-Making." In *Advances in Librarianship,* ed. Wesley Simonton, vol. 13, 2–47. New York: Academic Press, 1984.

McClure, Charles R. "A View from the Trenches: Costing and Performance Measures for Academic Library Public Services." *College and Research Libraries* 47, no. 4 (1986): 323–36.

McClure, Charles, and Betsy Reifsnyder. "Performance Measures for Corporate Information Centers." *Special Libraries* 75, no. 3 (1984): 193–204.

McGrath, William E. "Correlating the Subjects of Books Taken Out of and Books Used with an Open-Stack Library." *College and Research Libraries* 32, no. 4 (1971): 280–85.

Metz, Paul, and Charles A. Litchfield. "Measuring Collections Use at Virginia Tech." *College and Research Libraries* 49, no. 6 (1988): 501–13.

Mills, Peter K., Richard B. Chase, and Newton Margulies. "Motivating the Client/Employee System as a Service Production Strategy." *Academy of Management Review* 8, no. 2 (1983): 301–10.

Molyneux, Robert E. ACRL *University Library Statistics 1987–88.* Chicago: American Library Association, 1989.

Murfin, Marjorie. "National Reference Measurement: What Can It Tell Us about Staffing?" *College and Research Libraries* 44, no. 5 (1983): 321–33.

Murfin, Marjorie E., and Gary M. Gugelchuk. "Development and Testing of a Reference Transaction Assessment Instrument." *College and Research Libraries* 48, no. 4 (1987): 314–38.

National Center for Education Statistics, Education Division. *Library Statistics of Colleges and Universities: Institutional Data* (LIBGIS III/HEGIS XII). Washington, D.C., 1977.

Olson, Lina M. "Reference Service Evaluation in Medium-Sized Academic Libraries: A Model." *Journal of Academic Librarianship* 9, no. 6 (1984): 322–29.

Orr, R. H. "Measuring the Goodness of Library Services: A General Framework for Considering Quantitative Measures." *Journal of Documentation* 29, no. 3 (1973): 315–32.

Orr, Richard H., Vern M. Pings, Irwin H. Pizer, and Edwin E. Olson. "Development of Methodological Tools for Planning and Managing Library Services: I. Project Goals and Approach." *Bulletin of the Medical Library Association* 56, no. 3 (1968): 235–40.

Orr, Richard H., Vern M. Pings, Irwin H. Pizer, Edwin E. Olson, and Carol C. Spencer. "Development of Methodological Tools for Planning and Managing Library Services: II. Measuring a Library's Capability for Procuring Documents." *Bulletin of the Medical Library Association* 56, no. 3 (1968a): 241–67.

Powell, Ronald R. "Reference Effectiveness: A Review of Research." *Library and Information Science Research* 6, no. 1 (1984): 3-20.

Powell, Ronald R. *The Relationship of Library User Studies to Performance Measures: A Review of the Literature.* Champaign-Urbana: University of Illinois Graduate School of Library and Information Science, 1988.

Ralli, Tony. "Performance Measures for Academic Libraries." *Australian Academic and Research Libraries* 18, no. 1 (1987): 1–9.

Revill, Don H. "Availability' as a Performance Measure for Academic Libraries." *Journal of Librarianship* 19, no. 1 (1987): 14–30.

Rohde, Nancy Freeman. "Information Needs." In *Advances in Librarianship*, ed. Wesley Simonton, vol. 14, 49–73. New York: Academic Press, 1986.

Rothstein, Samuel. "The Measurement and Evaluation of Reference Service." *Library Trends* 12, no. 3 (1964): 456–72.

Rubin, Richard. *In-House Use of Materials in Public Libraries.* Urbana-Champaign: University of Illinois Graduate School of Library and Information Science, 1986.

Rzasa, Philip V., and Norman R. Baker. "Measures of Effectiveness for a University Library." *Journal of the American Society for Information Science* 23, no. 4 (1972): 248–53.

Schrader, Alvin M. "Performance Standards for Accuracy in Reference and Information Services: The Impact of Unobtrusive Measurement Methodology." *Reference Librarian*, no. 11 (Fall/Winter 1984): 197–214.

Schwartz, Diane G., and Dottie Eakin. "Reference Service Standards, Performance Criteria, and Evaluation." *Journal of Academic Librarianship* 12, no. 1 (1986): 4–8.

Shaughnessy, Thomas W. "The Search for Quality." *Journal of Library Administration* 8, no. 1 (1987): 5–10.

Streatfield, D. "Moving Towards the Information User: Some Research and Its Implications." *Social Science Information Studies* 3, no. 4 (1983): 223–40.

Suchman, Edward A. *Evaluative Research: Principles and Practice in Public Service and Social Action Programs.* New York: Russell Sage Foundation, 1967.

Swanson, Rowena W., and Joseph Mayer. "Performing Evaluation Studies in Information Science." *Journal of the American Society for Information Science* 26, no. 3 (1975): 140–56.

Swisher, Robert, and Charles R. McClure. *Research for Decision Making: Methods for Librarians.* Chicago: American Library Association, 1984.

Swift, Donald F., Viola A. Will, and Dawn A. Bramer. "A Sociological Approach to the Design of Information Systems." *Journal of the American Society for Information Science* 30, no. 4 (1979): 215–23.

Tagliacozzo, Renata. "Estimating the Satisfaction of Information Users." *Bulletin of the Medical Library Association* 65, no. 2 (1977): 243–48.

Taylor, Colin R. "A Practical Solution to Weeding University Library Periodicals Collections." *Collection Management* 1, no. 3/4 (1976/77): 27–45.

Tessier, Judith A., Wayne W. Crouch, and Pauline Atherton. "New Measures of User

Satisfaction with Computer-Based Literature Searches." *Special Libraries* 68, no. 11 (1977): 383–89.

Tolle, John E., Nancy P. Sanders, and Neal K. Kaske. "Determining the Required Number of Online Catalog Terminals: A Research Study." *Information Technology and Libraries* 2, no. 3 (1983): 261–65.

Tufte, Edward R. *The Visual Display of Quantitative Information*. Cheshire, Conn.: Graphics Press, 1983.

Van House, Nancy A. "In Defense of Fill Rates." *Public Libraries* 27, no. 1 (Spring, 1988b): 25–27.

Van House, Nancy A. "Output Measures: Some Lessons from Baltimore County." *Public Libraries* 24, no. 3 (Fall, 1985): 102–5.

Van House, Nancy A. "Public Library Effectiveness: Theory, Measures, and Determinants." *Library and Information Science Research* 8, no. 3 (1986): 261–83.

Van House, Nancy A. "A Response to D'Elia." *Public Libraries* 27, no. 1 (1988a): 32–33.

Van House, Nancy A. "A Time Allocation Theory of Public Library Use." *Library and Information Science Research* 5, no. 4 (1983): 365–84.

Van House, Nancy A., Mary Jo Lynch, Charles R. McClure, Douglas L. Zweizig, and Eleanor Jo Rodger. *Output Measures for Public Libraries: A Manual of Standardized Procedures*. 2d ed. Chicago: American Library Association, 1987.

Van House, Nancy A., and Thomas Childers. "Unobtrusive Evaluation of a Reference Referral Network: The California Experience." *Library and Information Science Research* 6, no. 3 (1984): 305–19.

Wall, T. "Frequency Distributions of Recorded Use for Students Using Academic Library Collections." *Collection Management* 6, no. 3/4 (1985): 11–24.

Webster, Duane E. "Choices Facing Academic Libraries in Allocating Scarce Resources." In *Library Budgeting: Critical Challenges for the Future*, ed. Sul H. Lee, 75–87. Ann Arbor, Mich.: Pierian Press, 1977.

Weech, Terry L., and Herbert Goldhor. "Obtrusive versus Unobtrusive Evaluation of Reference Service in Five Illinois Public Libraries: A Pilot Study." *Library Quarterly* 52, no. 4 (1982): 305–24.

Wenger, Charles B., and Judith Childress. "Journal Evaluation in a Large Research Library." *Journal of the American Society for Information Science* 28, no. 5 (1977): 293–99.

White, G. Travis. "Quantitative Measures of Library Effectiveness." *Journal of Academic Librarianship* 3, no. 3 (1977): 128–36.

White, Howard. "Measurement at the Reference Desk." *Drexel Library Quarterly* 17, no. 1 (1981): 3–35.

Whiteley, Sandy. *ACRL University Library Statistics, 1983–1984*. Chicago: Association of College and Research Libraries, 1985.

Whitlatch, Jo Bell. "Client/Service Provider Perceptions of Service Outcomes in Academic Libraries: Effects of Feedback and Uncertainty." Berkeley: University of California Ph.D. diss., 1987.

Whitlatch, Jo Bell. "Unobtrusive Studies and the Quality of Academic Library Reference Services." *College and Research Libraries* 50, no. 2 (1989): 181–94.

Wilson, T. D. "A Case Study in Qualitative Research?" *Social Science Information Studies* 1, no. 4 (1981b): 241–46.

Wilson, T. D. "On User Studies and Information Needs." *Journal of Documentation* 37, no. 1 (1981a): 3–15.

Wilson, T. D., and D. R. Streatfield. "Information Needs in Local Authority Social Services Departments: An Interim Report on Project INISS." *Journal of Documentation* 33, no. 4 (1977): 277–93.

Wilson, T. D., and D. R. Streatfield. "Structured Observation in the Investigation of

Information Needs." *Social Science Information Studies* 1, no. 3 (1981): 173–84.

Wilson, T. D., D. R. Streatfield, and C. Mullings. "Information Needs in Local Authority Social Services Departments: A Second Report on Project INISS." *Journal of Documentation* 35, no. 2 (1979): 120–36.

Zweizig, Douglas, and Eleanor Jo Rodger. *Output Measures for Public Libraries.* Chicago: American Library Association, 1982.

INDEX

Prepared by Carol R. Kelm

Nancy A. Van House received her Ph.D. from the School of Library and Information Studies, University of California, Berkeley, where she is currently an associate professor. She is the principal author of *Output Measures for Public Libraries* (2nd edition) and co-author of *Planning and Role Setting for Public Libraries*, published by the American Library Association in 1987. She was co-principal investigator on the Public Library Effectiveness Study, which has resulted in several reports and journal articles, and has published numerous articles and books. Her current research focuses on the academic libraries.

Beth T. Weil received her M.L.S. from the University of California, Berkeley, where she is currently Head Librarian, BioSciences Library. Her previous positions include Head Librarian of the Berkeley Library and of the Falconer Biology Library at Stanford University. She was also a reference librarian and a library associate at the National Library of Medicine.

Charles R. McClure completed his Ph.D. at Rutgers University and is currently professor of Information Studies at Syracuse University. He was principal investigator on the Public Library Development Project and co-author of *Planning and Role Setting for Public Libraries* and *Output Measures for Public Libraries*. More recently, he has directed projects related to U.S. government information policy for the U.S. Congress, Office of Technology Assessment, and the Government Printing Office. He has numerous monographs, reports, chapters, and papers. He has also served as a consultant to academic, public, special, and school libraries as well as to a number of public agencies and private corporations.